Handbook for
Fairy Godmothers

Transforming Our Lives Through Loving

Diana Spirithawk, DSS

Co-Published by
Leverage Press/Hybrid Global Publishing
301 E 57th Street, 4th fl
New York, NY 10022

Manufactured in the United States of America,
or in the United Kingdom when distributed elsewhere.

Author Diana Spirithawk, DSS
Handbook for Fairy Godmothers: Transforming Our Lives Through Loving

ISBN: Paperback: 978-1-938015-67-0
ISBN: eBook: 978-1-938015-68-7

Cover design by: Joe Potter
Interior design: Scribe Inc.

Dedication

For my beautiful husband, David, who loves and
supports me unconditionally, who knows my true heart,
who inspires me daily and has given me a loving home.

For my two great-grand-daughters, Traci and Samantha,
who are the jewels in my Fairy Godmother crown. You inspire
me to want a new world full of beauty and goodness for you.

For my spiritual mentor, John-Roger, I would not have
made it without your divine love and guidance,
and John Morton, my blessings man.

For my friends and spiritual sisters who have
always been there for me, Snowy Owl Woman and
Beloved Pamela. Thank God for your healing friendship.

Table of Contents

Introduction

"No act of kindness, no matter how small, is ever wasted."

~ AESOP

Where would Cinderella be without her Fairy Godmother? Could she have married her handsome prince without the intervention of a Fairy Godmother? Her world changed with a little help from a kindly, understanding patroness waving a magic wand and sprinkling her magical powers and fairy dust throughout the kingdom to ensure that Cinderella attend the ball with all its fineries. Ultimately, a Fairy Godmother made all the difference in Cinderella's world.

While many children might know a bit about Fairy Godmothers from stories and Disney movies, adults tend to forget the magic that made them believe at one time that everything is possible. This is one of the reasons that I wrote my book. I sincerely believe that there are Fairy Godmothers everywhere as well as Fairy Godfathers. I like to refer to them as "Beary" Godfathers because they are gentle, protective, and comforting just like a favorite teddy bear. As a Fairy Godmother, I see my role as mentoring and providing guidance wherever the need arises and, if I'm lucky, I can spread a little fun-loving magic. We could all use a little more fun and loving in this world. While I don't fly around on a set of wings or claim to have a magic wand, I do have a good imagination and the desire to create sparkles of love-light and magical possibilities wherever I am.

A non-believer told me once that being a Fairy Godmother or "Beary" Godfather is silly and why should we care about them? Because where there is a Fairy Godmother, there is light-heartedness and magical possibilities. I believe in magic, the magic of "a world full of loving and peace." That is the best reason I know to have more of us around. In fact, I believe there should be many, many more, at least two on every block in every neighborhood.

What is the persona of a Fairy Godmother? Some religions call for having a godparent named for the birth and blessing of every child. Many of us never had that spiritual possibility fulfilled. Fairy Godmothers know that it's never too late to have a happy childhood and to know that we are precious and loved. When I am asked, "What do you do?" I reply, "I am a Fairy Godmother," and I see the recognition in their eyes and a touching into their hearts. Fairy Godmothers represent, in every psyche, the return to a sense of innocence and wonder from when we were four or five years old. As adults, we must do "adult" things to run this world and our lives, but without the Fairy godmothers around to remind us, we have a world terribly bereft of the magic of innocence and wonder. It's never too late to believe in the power of love, is it?

Surely, you know that warm and fuzzy feeling when you participate or even observe an act of kindness. In both instances, it makes for a better person just because of the spiritual energy that is exchanged between both people not to mention the health benefits. From time to time, everyone needs a hand up otherwise our hopes and dreams might never materialize.

Sadly, many people in our world are only looking out for number one and could care less about the well-being of the people around them. I think these people are misdirected. I see them as missing out on life and lacking the sense of well-being that comes from the simple joy of selfless service. They've lost the wonder of everyday miracles and especially the opening of their own hearts. Many have become insensitive, righteous, and self-involved, hence the increase in the bullying phenomenon and other hateful acts. Some hold back from showing goodwill because they don't want to appear "soft," and may even be too wrapped up in fear and negativity or may even just be shy.

Are you Fairy Godmother or "Beary" Godfather material? Do you have a twinkle in your eye and a passion in your heart to infuse the world with hope regardless of race, religion, gender, circumstance or situation? I believe that we are all highly creative and loving by nature and when we don't give ourselves an outlet to express those parts of ourselves, it suppresses our enthusiasm for life.

We need to spread the idea that the more we give, the richer we become. What could be better than uniting a community through charity, good deeds, self-less acts of service or a cheerful attitude to "lighten up" someone's life.

Won't you join us in making our world a better place? When we allow ourselves to be led by love as our guiding principle, then kindness becomes the antidote for all the bad stuff. You already possess the magic to be part of the change. What greater gift can you share with someone than your open heart? The ultimate gift is the gift of yourself.

We all have the capacity to cultivate peace, harmony and beauty in our world one person at a time and this book is your "magic wand" to help you to open your heart to a more loving world. Living a life of showing genuine kindness is a gradual process of purposeful words and actions. The first steps will be to change self-neglect into self-love and then you will be able to fall in love with the world around you.

One way to make use of the material in this book is to read it through once, then go through it again. Use the questions to deepen your experience and the affirmations to support you in your transformation. As we embrace ourselves as the Beloved we already are, then the world around us will transform. This is how the world will be made beautiful and peaceful. I wish you all the success possible in your quest for more love in your life and in our world. Allow me to take you on a journey of love and self-enlightenment. Won't you take my hand in this timeless effort to be someone's Fairy Godmother or "Beary" Godfather?

Chapter 1

The Modern Day Fairy Godmother

"What the world needs now is love sweet love,
no not just for some, but for everyone."

~ HAL DAVID AND BURT BACHARACH

What are the qualities of a modern day Fairy Godmother and why do we still have a need for them in today's modern world? Certainly they are only the stuff of fantasy and imagination, right? Surely, today we are too sophisticated to believe in such things let alone behave like one, right? If that were true, that Fairy Godmothers are unnecessary make-believe characters, then why has so much been written about them in mythic studies, dream work, and have been shared through stories for hundreds of years, not to mention what Disney has created with them.

I looked **fairy** up in a children's dictionary and it says, ". . . an imaginary person with magical powers." According to Wikipedia, Fairy Godmother, is defined as, *"A fairy with magical powers that acts as a mentor or parent, taking the role sometimes of what an actual Godparent might play."* Wherever there is sadness, turmoil, loneliness, feelings of inadequacy, fearfulness, there is a need for a Fairy Godmother.

Fairies are not fantasies, they are magical and their magic is the magic of LOVE, which I think the world needs more than anything else, don't you? Do you remember the stage play of "Peter Pan?" There was a scene where Captain Hook poisoned Tinkerbell. Tink's light began to fade. She was dying. Peter Pan turned to the audience and said, "She's going to die unless we do something. Clap your hands! Clap your hands and say, 'I believe in fairies'. . . ." Miraculously, Tinkerbell heard everyone clapping and her light reappeared.

If fairies are to be a real and powerful force for good, it depends on you and me and whether we have the courage to step outside of our comfort zone and share our light and love with the world around us through random acts of loving, caring, sharing, and kindness.

Fairy "Godmothering" is a two-fold endeavor. The first part is to find and foster the "Beloved" within ourselves, one of the words that describes the Soul, God within. You cannot give away love if you can't find it in yourself so this book is not only about giving love, but it is about embracing ourselves as the Beloved and loving ourselves so well that we have an overflow of love to give to the world. The Beloved within us is as close as our next breath and we have but to connect with the love we are. The second is to take that love within us and find ways to express it, giving it away, as in the words of this song.

"Love is the strangest thing that I know,
you keep it around by letting it go,
and you follow close and you follow slow and
love will take you where love wants to go . . ."

~ MICHAEL SUN, UNFINISHED LOVE SONG FROM
"SONGS FOR THE LOVING HEART"

This kind of love is not grasping, controlling or willful. It is free flowing, pure, and unconditional. It can be as simple as reaching out to give someone a hand with their groceries, smiling at a child, saying good morning to a stranger, giving a pat on the back or a friendly wave, stopping to admire a garden or someone's pet. Simple kindnesses like giving your attention to someone can make a person's day. You might be the only one the person talks to all day long. Our world is so fast-paced that we scarcely have time to connect with our neighbors let alone the senior that lives at the end of the block.

So, the art of being a Fairy Godmother/Beary Godfather, is taking the time to connect to the Beloved within ourselves, to look for it in others and to see through the eyes of love. A healthy dose of looking for the humor in life's everyday experiences doesn't hurt either, besides laughter is healthy.

Here are some of the qualities of a Fairy Godmother from the word FAIRY.

F   Fearless—Faith
A   Awareness—Acceptance
I   Intention—Inspiration
R   Right Timing—Risking
Y   You, saying "yes" to love

We are going to take a closer look now at each of these qualities and explore the attributes of how each of us can become a Fairy Godmother and a force for the good.

Chapter 2

F ~ Fearless and Faithful

"Faith is the only thing I know of that is stronger than fear."

~ Joyce Meyer

A Fairy Godmother has to be **fearless** in her resolution to extend herself and open her heart to new people and circumstances. She must have **faith** in her ability to love even if she doesn't know the person in front of her. What is the love of a Fairy Godmother? It is unconditional, positive, and always looking for the good in people. That's all she has to remember. Love is like our attention and it will go wherever you send it. Physically, its center is in the area of the heart. It can show up through a loving touch, through our eyes as a loving compassionate look, a kind voice, and always it is a choice. I have found that as I lean into a loving attitude, I am pulled into its greater expression.

A Fairy Godmother could be out shopping and see a mother with a squalling baby. She might look at the baby and the mother and smile with a loving expression and say something comforting by bringing her inner peace and knowingness that everything's going to be all right. If she's too afraid to open up to a "stranger," she won't have the nerve to extend a simple expression. She has to have faith in the power of love and that just by her willingness and sheer intention, love and encouragement can be expressed to change the energy, ease tensions. Maybe the mother needs some attention, also.

The word fear has its own message: False Evidence Appearing Real. She does not give into false evidence, but takes the initiative and reaches out, gently, to do something uplifting. She must keep her faith in the power of loving even if the only thing she can do is place a blessing of light and love from her heart on to another person or situation. According to James 2:14 KJV: "Faith without works is dead." What are the Fairy Godmother's works of faith? It's seeing the person as precious without judgment. A simple smile or kind word, a comment redirecting a sad thought into a hopeful outcome and compassionately listening to the feelings as they spill over. Ask them what they really want, create an invitation into a bigger more loving positive idea of their life, encourage inner strength, and remind them of their special gifts, abilities, and talents. Never give up on the faith that they are whole and complete regardless of the person's circumstances.

Have you ever encountered a person who had an amazing talent and yet didn't realize the gift that he/she has? Despite their denial, you just kept seeing them through the eyes of love, seeing their gifts, acknowledging them, praying for them to recognize their own beauty and strength and whatever their specialness is. Then, one day, maybe even months or years later, you run into the person again and see them expressing that gift. Maybe the person even tells you that it seemed crazy to say what you did, but over time they kept thinking about it and how encouraging you were, believing in them and finally they took a risk. Finally, the person opened up and stepped into the vision that you held for them. You were their Fairy Godmother at that time. You saw something true and valuable in them even though they couldn't. Often, we can't always see our own gifts clearly.

Sometimes, we as Fairy Godmothers can only hold for a person, sending silent prayers of love and encouragement because that person is not accessible, for whatever reason. That is where faith plays a role, as we set the goodness in motion, inside of ourselves, it will, by holding the vision, find its target. And, we always ask *for the highest good of all* making room for divine perfection.

I knew a woman whose daughter turned to drugs at a very young age. The daughter had children that one by one were taken into the safety of their fathers. The daughter was left with only one of her children, a little girl. By then, they were homeless due to drugs being her top priority and the disease had rendered the daughter incapable of working. The welfare system was so overloaded that this problem continued to fall through the cracks. The grandmother had attempted to provide a home for her daughter and granddaughter, but because of the drug use, she too had actually lost two places to live because of her daughters actions. People would ask the mother why she bothered at all, that she had lost enough through the daughter's dysfunction. The mother persisted with the vision that one day her daughter would get better even though the professionals warned against it. She continued to look for the two of them and would take food to them or take them to a restaurant, always treating them with love and kindness, but also knowing that she couldn't take them in again because of the drugs.

Finally, the daughter went to jail and the granddaughter went to foster care enabling the mother to spend more time with the granddaughter. The daughter was released from jail having been diagnosed as bi-polar with orders to stay drug free. The mother waited and watched her daughter, continuing the vigilance of holding the picture of her daughters' true nature. As time went by and healing took place, the daughter got clean and sober and 11 years later, she is an honest, responsible, and caring woman who is helping her own daughter with her little family. This woman demonstrated faith regardless of what the outer circumstances were. She knew her daughters true nature and that underneath all the drama and drugs, healing and wholeness would prevail. She nurtured this vision of wholeness with loving kindness and never wavered. She kept the **faith** undaunted until the truth was a reality. She **was fearless in her dream for her daughter** despite what others said and despite what the current circumstances looked like.

A Fairy Godmother must be **fearless** in her intention to bring about the truth and power of love. Often, she must have the **faith** of a mustard seed, choosing to see the true beauty and preciousness of a person. We don't have to know anything about a person, when we are operating with faith. We just hold the positive vision that all will be fine. Sometimes, the turn of events is for the growth of a person and they will grow as a result or make some change. We can't always see the big picture, but we operate from the greater truth that we can at least do something to comfort and encourage. Sometimes, the Fairy Godmother is the only one with faith in a person until the divine unfolds.

A Fairy Godmother must know that her ability to hold the vision of the positive can and does bring about small miracles of perfect timing so always ask for the highest good of all concerned. As you hold the vision of good, the vision of good will hold you in its loving grace and you'll see not only the possibility of good coming your way, but feel the good inside you.

Our affirmation for this chapter:
I am courageous and free and all fear melts in the face of my loving.

Questions to deepen your awareness:
1. Have you ever had a fear that you overcame? What helped you overcome the fear?
2. Are you ready to embrace yourself with love? What would that look like? If not what stands in your way?
3. Write in your journal about a fear that never came to pass.

Chapter 3

A ~ Awareness and Acceptance

*"Out beyond the ideas of wrongdoing and rightdoing
there is a field. I'll meet you there."*

~ Rumi

A Fairy Godmother has inner and outer **awareness** of what is going on around her in terms of where a smile, an encouraging word or a helping hand is needed. She is aware of her own feelings, her energy, her need for self-love and care and delivers it. She is aware of the need for love wherever it reveals itself.

To the Fairy Godmother, awareness is about how do I bring in more love for myself as well as others? One of the best ways I know to enhance more awareness is through the art of appreciation. Start looking around you for things to appreciate about other people, situations, i.e., seeing the glass half full instead of half empty. Nothing breaks the ice when meeting someone for the first time than finding something you appreciate about that person. It could be their hair, the shirt or dress they're wearing, how well they navigate the crowds, their smile, the eyes, etc.

Everyone has some special quality or expertise that is visible and let's not forget self-appreciation. When having a bad start to your day, sit down and make a list of what you appreciate about yourself, your life, and your accomplishments. Keep a journal of those moments when you make that connection as a Fairy Godmother; those random acts of kindness, loving, caring, and sharing. Write down the experiences and how it felt. When something happens that seems to miss your target of service, write down how you felt about it and WITHOUT judgment! The act of making notes and writing stories about our experiences helps us to see ways to improve and be more successful, such as overcoming shyness, developing sensitivity and nourishing our ability to accept ourselves and others. Stories are very healing. When you have that "down day," get your self-appreciation journal and read something good about yourself and restart your day.

A Fairy Godmother is **accepting** of herself and others. She knows that acceptance doesn't mean that she agrees, but that acceptance can prepare the way for change and transformation. In order to bring about transformation, she must accept what is, as it is, and then construct and hold a vision of the greater good always keeping in mind that God's will be done. Of course, we don't always know what God has in store for us or the object of our caring, but holding an uplifting vision is always better than the doom and gloom of worst case scenario. Whenever we hold a vision of good, we are embracing the God in the circumstance so even asking for grace for another person or situation can be a moment of transformation. The Fairy Godmother sees and accepts that there is preciousness in every human being and looks for signs of it. Also, acceptance is a natural demonstration of loving.

In the early 1990s, I was traveling between California and Arizona delivering my art to Sedona. I had forgotten to post my temporary license sticker in the window of my car so I was stopped and because Arizona had just opened a new women's prison, I was to be their guest and my car was impounded. (I had also forgotten about an old traffic ticket). I was put in a 20 by 40 foot cell with several other women ranging from DUI, drug use and sales, and "ladies" of the night. Needless to say, this was not my usual community. I was a grandmother, artist, and spiritual seeker after all. My usual travels were to spiritual camps where I studied and participated with the "Good Red Road"—a term for someone learning and living the Native American spiritual ways besides delivering and selling my ceremonial art.

As I sat in the corner on the floor of the cell with my legs curled under me, I surveyed my fellow inmates. I was pretty scared. I'd seen the movies about violence in prisons, although I was only in a holding cell. It was crowded and I couldn't help but notice that all the bunks were inhabited by the biggest and angriest of the group.

I felt compelled to call upon the "light" and "love" of God to protect me, lest I open my mouth at the wrong time. The floor was hard and cold. A young woman, thin and pretty came up to me and sat down next to me on the floor. She introduced herself and to my surprise, she asked my name and then began to tell me her life story. I learned that she was one of the "ladies." She was sweet, sincere, open, and some of what she shared was heart rendering. I knew that she lived in a completely different world than I did, even though we were both women, both white, both had experiences with the opposite sex. The thought, "There but for the grace of God go I," was floating around in my head. She opened my heart with her tender story, we hugged and then she moved on.

Shortly afterwards, another "lady" sat down next to me and poured out her heart. During this time, I just listened without judging, but with concerned compassion. This went on for awhile as a total of six girls sat down to share with me. Each woman hugged me and then moved on. I did notice that I was getting warm nods from the other women and realized I had nothing to fear.

After sitting on the floor for several hours, a social worker came in and finally took me to a single holding room until the next day when I was able to make bail, locate my car and continue on with my business.

Yes, at first glance, I was kicking myself around the block for my stupidity and the senseless trouble I created for myself, but I soon began to realize that God decided to make good use of my "incarceration" and pressed me into service by giving me another plan, which was to give my unconditional love to those beautiful women. That was a Fairy Godmother working in the moment if ever there was one, long before I even knew or entertained the idea.

We as Fairy Godmothers are sometimes sent to places, people and their circumstances when we least expect it. Now when I think of those women, I still have a sense of warmth that they trusted to me. I was a stranger to them and their world and yet I had an unconditional love for them. I still send them the Light and ask that they find grace in their lives even though I've forgotten their names and faces. I never forgot the love we shared in the form of true **acceptance**.

The opposite of acceptance is judgment. Like many formal definitions, judgment has several meanings. My definition is *to criticize or condemn someone or some circumstance from a position of assumed moral superiority* whereas the definition of acceptance is *the willingness to tolerate a difficult idea, opinion, a difficult or unpleasant situation or person.*

"Love is the absence of judgment."

~ DALAI LAMA

We as Fairy Godmothers have to accept ourselves, good, bad or something in between. What if we were to drop the whole idea of good or bad and just accept what is. There are things we do or have done, habits, for example, that created less than what we really want. So, if we look at it all as learning and growing, we dispense completely with the idea of judgment in any form and we move instead into acceptance. In the clarity of acceptance, we open ourselves up to new possibilities of transforming our lives and the world around us. Judgment holds us to the past and keeps our creative mind from expanding our reality and all the good that is possible.

Another aspect of acceptance is the quality of listening; truly listening and not going anywhere else in your head, but just listening to what a person has to say can be extremely healing.

> *"Listening is one of the deepest, most profound signs of loving . . .*
> *listening to yourself and listening to others. Your heart goes out and*
> *wraps around them and Gods Spirit of loving embraces you both."*
>
> ~ JOHN-ROGER, DSS

Our affirmation for this chapter:
I am loving and accepting of myself just as I am. I am precious.

Questions to deepen your awareness:
1. What does it mean to you to be precious?
2. What quality or habit do you have that needs acceptance?
3. What is one thing you can forgive about your life or yourself? Write about an experience you have had of unconditional love, for yourself and someone else.

Chapter 4

I ~ Inspiration and Intention

*"When you are inspired . . . dormant forces, faculties
and talents become alive, and you discover yourself to be a
greater person by far than you ever dreamed yourself to be."*

~ PATANJALI

Out of all the definitions for **inspiration,** I like author and speaker, Wayne Dyer's best. He saw inspiration as a "living in-spirit." Other spiritual texts refer to inspiration as "fire from God." Webster's Dictionary tells us that **inspiration** is *"a prompting, especially to creative action that arises within the mind, an illumination, divine influence."* Another dictionary describes it as *"to influence, move, or guide by divine or supernatural inspiration; to exert an animating, enlivening, or exalting influence on."* When I am inspired, I feel a welling up of love, joy, peace and inner knowing in my heart, all at the same time.

The Fairy Godmother fuels her "divine fire" by looking for inspiration in books, movies, music, words of wisdom, even affirmations that inspire and lift her up. She can find inspiration by spending time in nature, being still, meditating, praying as well as doing random acts of kindness. She can ask God for inspiration as well as answers that will guide her. She gathers stories for inspiration so she is able to pass it along knowing that a good story can lift someone to higher levels of hope and understanding in times of self-doubt or discouragement. Music can be highly inspirational and heart opening. Stevie Nicks of Fleetwood Mac says that she was always surrounded by music that inspired her . . . *"inspired people don't stay down."*

Inspiration is a two-way street and we must be open to it. For example, giving and receiving appreciation can spark an awakening. When someone reaches out to us through acts of kindness, our appreciation for their actions can enhance their desire to inspire others to continue to do more because it makes them feel good. Feeling good is feeling God and God's energy inspires, opens our hearts, which is a very natural thing for Fairy Godmothers, don't you think?

A few years ago, a scientific study was conducted by a university where they measured the level of serotonin released into a person's system when the recipient performed an act of kindness. Further investigation revealed that not only was the receiver of the kindness impacted, so was the giver. They also discovered that even a bystander observing the exchange of an act of kindness between two people received enhanced levels of serotonin in their blood stream. Serotonin is one of the primary "happy" chemicals in the body and it raises the immune response. Feeling happy and emotionally uplifted is a heart action—the action that leads to "inspiration."

One of the things that inspires me is when I see someone reaching out to another whose path seems full of problems and adversities and they extend a helping hand, making a difference in a life. Inspiring stories can lift us up and give us hope when the situations otherwise seem hopeless. Inspiration to me is when we are lifted out of everyday experiences and find reasons to believe in the beauty and power of good and then we connect more consciously to the God within.

What inspires you? I like to keep track of things that inspire me such as a poem, favorite books, certain melodies and lyrics, affirmations, and more. There may be people in your life who inspire you or sweet memories that you treasure because they made you feel warm inside and, if you're lucky, maybe you also have a story about how you inspired someone else to change course or follow another path.

An inspiring story that resonates with me occurred when I was a young mother struggling with four children under the age of six. To make ends meet, I occasionally got jobs (before the Internet) performing as a clown at children's birthday parties. I sang and told stories with puppets. One Saturday, I attended a spiritual festival where we were all encouraged to share our gifts and talents with our spiritual community. Dressed like a clown, I had taken my guitar and had a few puppets in my pockets. I wandered throughout the group telling stories and singing songs and sharing my puppets with the kids.

There was a teenage girl about 15 years old who I sang to and showed her how the puppets worked. Even though she was a teenager, she seemed to really enjoy it and proceeded to sing along and talk to the puppets. The girl was somewhat awkward socially, but we had a glorious time. Years later, I saw her at another spiritual event and she came up to me and showed me her cards. She too had become a clown and even advertised her services in the "yellow pages" (which was long ago) and she was able to support herself doing this. I thought to myself, "Wow, what a perfect expression for this soul." She then said to me, "It was all because of you." I was stunned. She went on to say that she tried beauty school, but it hadn't worked out. She said, "I thought of you and how much fun we had that day, long ago, so I got a costume, practiced children's jokes and collected some puppets, learned a list of children's songs, and now it is my career." I was humbled by her comment that I had inspired her and now she had become someone she was truly proud of.

I am so grateful and inspired that she found her true calling and I was able to help her. We don't always know the full extent of how we impact people around us, but each act of kindness or selfless service that we extend into the world, each acknowledgement, appreciation, enriches and ultimately brings more love into the world. Multiply my simple sharing by 1000 and over the years it results in millions of inspiring moments. Now, that is truly bringing more love into the world. We can't feel angry, resentful or negative when we are inspired. They just don't coexist.

Encouragement of others is something everyone can give. Everybody needs what you have to give such as a listening ear, open arms or words of encouragement. It may be your smile that uplifts a sad heart, a story that gives someone hope, a different perspective. Believe in the power of love because your expressions of love inspire more positive actions. Who doesn't want to feel the exhilaration of inspiration, this is your time to shine.

What if our divine essence is determined by how much love we can give, receive, share, experience and generate? This is the magnificent being we can be and we can always discover new things about ourselves. If you feel called, feel curious, feel a sense of purpose at the prospect of wanting to see more love in the world, then you are being called to be a Fairy Godmother.

"When you focus on being a blessing, you'll always be blessed"

~ JOEL OLSTEEN

In Mazlo's *Hierarchy of Needs*, he states, *"What is necessary to change a person is to change their awareness of themselves."* To be inspired is to become more aware of yourself as a lovable, beautiful, capable being with a calling sent by the Divine.

One of the things that inspires me about Joseph Campbell's *The Heroes Journey* is something that we've seen in the movies or stories that we've read. If we look at our own life as a hero's journey, we might be surprised to see that even our own lives can be framed as heroic.

My hero's journey started when I was born into a family that was bereft of loving expressions, even the most basic ones like being touched, seen or heard. I felt very alienated by the one who was my first and most basic early relationship, my mother. She never showed me the usual expressions of loving. It's one thing to have no mother because she died or left and what a terrible tragedy for a child. But to have a mother in front of you that sees through you, as if you didn't exist, invisible, untouchable, this was my beginning. I wanted love for myself and my mother who was abandoned by her mother. As a little girl, I thought that if I loved her enough, then she would learn how to love me back, but that didn't happen until much later in our lives.

"The wound is the place where the light enters you"

~ RUMI

I could not consciously change my beginning, but I could and would create a better ending for my story, my life, my hero's journey.

While my early years were complicated, it served to create a deep longing, a conviction, that "what the world needs now is love sweet love" and since I lived as a young adult in the 1960s, the new songs of universal love were my emotional life, which ignited a desire to create more loving, caring, and sharing in the world. I'm confident that I am not alone in this desire, this intention. I believe there are others, possibly you who are reading this book, can see the vision I have for a more loving and gentle world. Wherever you are, whoever you are, join me in committing to more love in our world and then for fun, we can all become undercover Fairy Godmothers, disguised as housewives, teachers, retirees, young and old people alike of every color and shape. In fact, that's how it has to be doesn't it? We don't want to leave anyone out of this world of loving.

"Inspiration is intention obeyed."

~ EMILY CARR

The meaning of **intention**, according to Merriam-Webster says, "*intention is the thing that you plan to do or achieve: an aim or purpose.*" It means that you absolutely are committed to doing what you are intended to do. A Fairy Godmother has a clear intention about her business for channeling the flow of love into the world through her thoughts, feelings, vision, actions, and purpose. She is pure of heart in her intention to serve knowingly with a sense of fulfillment that promises to be the "frosting on the cake." She does "good" for the sake of goodness.

*"Go confidently in the direction of your
dreams, live the life you've imagined."*

~ HENRY DAVID THOREAU

So, in order to harness the power of intention, we know that visualization is one of the tools needed and actions with clear intention have power in them. When we act with peace and love, we are empowered to bring more of it into the world.

So we know that what we do in the name of "more love in the world" becomes our statement of purpose, our intention. Our purpose causes us to step out and take action, action that is powered by our goals to transform our world into a safer, happier, more blessed place. If we act as if it is happening, we can fearlessly venture out and continue with our acts of love, peace and kindness, trusting the process, and then by our sheer intention, our cause becomes a reality. We act, we trust, we let go, and let God.

Will we have moments when we lose our focus because we hear or see something on the nightly news that is contrary, some violence that has occurred in our town or neighborhood? This is bound to happen. Do we give up and give in to discouragement? No, the Fairy Godmother becomes even more determined to be the peace she seeks. She quietly reaches into herself and uses her visualization to see a picture that is one of harmony, peace, and unity. She breathes from her loving heart and she surrenders to inner peace.

She never deviates from the hope that something good will come out of every situation. Fairy Godmothers express love toward everyone they come in contact with, making a conscious effort to increase the acts of kindness as we go through our day. This to me is the real magic of love. The universe, being intelligent and conscious, makes it possible to affect the fabric of our world by our intention and the acts we do to create the intentions. Quantum physics makes the statement, "The universe rearranges itself to match your picture of reality." Funny how that works.

Fairy Godmothers in the fairy tales we read about are seen with magic wands and they recite magic words. What if our magic words became the focus and conviction to see a loving world and peaceful people, countries, cultures, all living in harmony with each other? We fuel this with our inner vision of how the world will look with even more love in it and we affirm it with affirmations.

In my life and work of seeking the Beloved, I find that God IS intention, so by aligning with the Beloved, I am aligning with God within me. Each and every soul's identity is love, joy, beauty, peace, light, compassion and kindness. With these qualities as her guiding focus, she is sustained, blessed, and victorious.

Wayne Dyer writes that intention shapes our lives. He identifies the power of intention, the all-creating universal mind of intention as being a field of energy, a force in the universe that allows the act of creation to take place and that we are all a part of that creative force. By aligning with the qualities of this creative flow, we can harness this power to create. He says that this power is marked by certain qualities. The qualities of being creative, kind, loving, beautiful, expanding endlessly, and abundantly and ever receptive to align ourselves with these qualities. This is how we connect to that power of intention and manifest our desired outcomes.

So to me, anyway you look at it, as you keep aligned with these qualities, you are expressing a soulfulness that is the hallmark of a Fairy Godmother.

One day as I was immersed in the writing process, I had to run to the bank. The intention of what I was writing about and why was very much with me. I arrived at the bank and as I started for the door, a man came up and opened the door for me. I smiled and thanked him. I did my ready teller thing and I was soon after headed for the door. He rushed over to open it again and this time he remarked, "Well, I guess I've done my good deed for the day!" I smiled and looked at him thoughtfully for a moment and then I told him that if he wanted to feel really good all day long that he could continue to do other acts of kindness and service throughout the day to maintain that "feel good" mentality. He stood there looking at me, and finally as I turned to go, he stopped me. He asked me where had I heard that. I told him it is in my book and then he asked, "Your book?" He asked the name of my book and when I gave him the title, *Handbook for Fairy Godmothers*, then I added and "Beary Godfathers." He laughed and said, "Can I buy the book. Do you have one with you?" I was touched by his openness and thought to myself, this is a Beary Godfather for sure. I explained that I was in the process of completing it and offered my email address. Prior to departing, he asked for a hug and a "selfie." We exchanged emails then he shared that he was leaving the country to be married to his sweetheart who was waiting for him in Thailand. I was so happy to hear his news. Such a precious open hearted man, truly a husband and a Beary Godfather to be.

This experience was a demonstration of my intention to spread the word of transforming our world through loving actions. My intention is to sell at least a million copies of my book so that my message will inspire others into acts of kindness and caring and sharing everywhere. I have no doubt that when the book comes out, he'll buy one and will share his experience with others. The power of intention is irresistible to the universe.

I am always planting the seeds as I go along, for loving, caring, sharing, and kindness. The Dali Lama states that "kindness is my religion." Now, there's a Beary Godfather for you. Not long ago, I was told of a YouTube.com clip that introduced me to another quote by the Dali Lama, "*The world will be transformed by the western woman.*" I learned about this from a wonderful teacher I worked with, Mary Morrisey, and later read it in an article by the Huffington Post, February 10, 2013.

I firmly believe that we Fairy Godmothers and Beary Godfathers have the potential to transform our world. As we learn more about how to love ourselves and create peace from within, use our intention sustained by inspiration, we can couple it with random acts of kindness, thoughtfulness, loving, caring and sharing. I hope you will join me with intention to follow your heart and keep inspired.

Our affirmations for this chapter:
I am a radiant being filled with joy and inspiration.

Questions to deepen your awareness:
1. What is your intention for being a Fairy Godmother now?
2. If God is intention, what new way of being do you want?
3. What inspires you in your everyday life?

Chapter 5

R ~ Right Timing and Risk

*"The universe is always speaking to us . . .
sending us little messages, causing coincidences
and serendipities, reminding us to stop, to look
around, to believe in something else, something more."*

~ NANCY THAYER

A Fairy Godmother trusts that she is in the **right place at the right time** and that there are no accidents in the universe. Even when things seem to be all wrong, she knows that these circumstances could be a catalyst for growth and change. She trusts the higher understanding that everything is as it should be and she lends a hand or a heartfelt attitude when needed to facilitate growth and greater possibilities. A simple act of kindness in the moment can do some real good in the world.

Sometimes an opportunity for kindness and Fairy Godmothering can pop up at a moment's notice. Once I found a dog on our street. I didn't know who it belonged to as there was no tag, so I called it, petted it, and sat with it for awhile. In a short time, I heard the owner calling her dog and there we sat on the curb, waiting, and knowing that all was well. We've all had those impulses, and so, when you are called to be of service to your world, your community, you will be guided.

Taking a **risk** can be a scary experience. What if we were to reach out to someone we never met before and offer assistance and the person were to pull back and refuse our help. Well, if we offered and it is declined, it is better than doing nothing. Risking can mean that we might offer a silent blessing of light and goodwill to a person or situation knowing that regardless of what's going on, an inner prayer of gratitude for the possibility of miracles is present. Another scary part of risking is the possibility of making a mistake, failing to accomplish desired results and then we reject ourselves through self-criticism. If you think about it, we know that life is full of risks on any given day. It is fear that cripples hope whereas hope can fuel the ability to step forward to serve, to take a risk. We've all heard the old adage, *"Nothing ventured is nothing gained."* That is another one of the limiting aspects of holding back and not risking.

> *"It's in every one of us to be wise, find your heart,*
> *open up both your eyes. We can all know everything*
> *without ever knowing why, it's in every one of us."*

~ CLIFF RICHARD

If you stay small and never take a risk, what will you accomplish? Remember faith? We must have faith to bring more love into our world and risk the petty rejections, inner and outer, and go for the gold. What is the gold in a Fairy Godmother? The blessings that come from acts of kindness and loving, compassionate attitudes and the simple joy of selfless service. We can have contentment and a sense of purpose, and fall asleep at night knowing we made a difference.

Remember my experience about being picked up by the highway patrol in Arizona and put in the new women's prison there? The trusting women I met that shared their stories nourished my soul. They didn't know me. I wasn't like them, in fact, I was much older than any of them. Do you think for one minute that when I woke up that morning, packed my car and headed to Sedona, that I had any idea of what fate had in store for me that day? This is a perfect example of being in the right place at the right time. Apparently, it was God's timing.

Speaking of right timing, it was two days before Christmas when I was driving home from a Christmas meditation. I lived in a somewhat rural community on the outskirts of a very affluent neighborhood. The San Antonio Parkway had just opened and went from where I was living to south Orange County just below the outermost foothills. The road was so new that empty lots preparing for new builds made up the scenery. There were hardly any turnarounds and almost no street lights along this ten mile lonely stretch of road. It was about 11:30 p.m. when I was returning home. I barely saw a man standing on the side of the road wildly waving his arms. Naturally, I wondered if he was all right, but it was also very late and very dark. As I passed him, my inner voice, intuition, said to go back and see if I could help. I had to drive another two miles to reach a turnaround and then back three miles to reach him along the side of the road.

My plan was to slow down, roll my window down, and talk to him first in order to feel out the situation. As soon as I stopped, I didn't have a chance to roll the window down. He opened the car door, jumped inside and slammed the door. The first thing I thought to do was to ask him if he was okay. He reached over and pinched me on the arm. I yelped and looked at him. He was looking at me intensely and said, "Can you see me?" I said that I could. He put his face in his hands and heaved a big sigh of relief. He said, "I fell asleep at the wheel of my truck and went off the road over an embankment." He said that he hit it so hard that the windshield shattered and fell away. He managed to climb through the windshield opening and got up to the road adding that he'd been out there for hours. He said that he kept waving at the few cars that came by, but no one stopped or acted like they even saw him. He figured that he must be dead, a ghost, which explained why no one stopped. "Thank you, thank you so much," he said. I told him that he was very much alive and I just wished he hadn't pinched me so hard. I then asked him where he lived and assured him that I'd drive him home. He continued to say how happy he was not to be dead. I guess you could say that I too was happy he wasn't dead since I was certain that I did not want to drive a ghost home.

I have had many moments when I found myself in the right place at the right time and it never ceases to amaze me. It is usually a very uplifting experience. Honestly, sometimes it can be very exhausting, but well worth the effort. You never know where or when you can make a difference in a person's life. It doesn't have to be on a big scale, or dangerous either. It can be simply giving someone asking for change a dollar bill and inwardly you are asking for them to be blessed with health, well-being and prosperity. No prayer goes unheard my Fairy Godmothers and Beary Godfathers. Sometimes, it comes back to you in mysterious and unexpected ways.

One year I was invited to northern California by a spiritual camp. As I was driving down the last five miles to the campground (before iPhones and before I could afford a GPS navigation system in my old car). I noticed that a raccoon had been hit by a car. As a student of Native American spiritual ways, traditionally it was customary to move the animal from the roadway and say a prayer over it while placing tobacco or blue cornmeal as a blessing on its journey to the beyond. I also noted a man walking with a huge pack on his back.

I decided to pull over and say the blessing for the soul of the raccoon and then I returned to my car. All life is connected so when you find an animal anywhere, you must honor it as its soul continues its life in the spirit world.

I then started having an inner dialogue about the man who continued to walk on. The intuitive part of me said to turn around and ask him if he needed a ride. The other side of my brain reminded me that he's a hiker. Hikers like to walk, they don't want rides. Needless to say, the "go back and see if he needs a ride" side won out and I turned around and drove back. I pulled over and he approached my window. I asked if he wanted a ride and he accepted. I also noticed that he wasn't a young person, at least older than I was at that time, possibly in his sixties. I was unfamiliar with the area and afraid that I could get lost, but when I told him where I was going he said it was just across the road from where he was going and he guided me. We talked about how long we were both staying and that our departure time and day were the same. I offered to drive him home provided it wasn't too far out of my way. He said that he'd like that.

So the weekend came to an end and I picked him up and drove him home. He told me how I could find my route home and for some reason he gave me his phone number "just in case," he said. About 30 miles down the road, my car broke down. This was before I could afford roadside car service, so I called him from a pay phone. He used his sister's AAA card to have my car towed to their mechanic and in three hours and $300 later, my car was repaired. I did not have the $300 to fix my car and struggled to find some solution for the problem. He waved my concerns away, paid it, and thanked me for my kindness to him. I thanked him and with a final hug, I drove away and never saw him again. I called him "walking man Bob". I did keep in touch with him for a while, to see how he was, which was always "all good." They say that "what goes around, comes around." Personally, I believe it is God taking care of us through each other. Now that I'm living my life as a Fairy Godmother, I can tell you with complete confidence that God does move in mysterious ways and he takes care of his Fairy Godmothers and Beary Godfathers.

The word **synchronicity** comes to my mind as I continue to write. In the 1920's Carl Gustav Jung, a Swiss Psychologist described the meaning of synchronicity as *"the experience of two or more events that are casually unrelated or unlikely to occur together by chance, yet are experienced as occurring together in a meaningful manner."* To me, by making myself available when called to be used by the spirit of God in the name of love and goodness a.k.a. a "Fairy Godmother," it is no less miraculous than the biblical story of the loaves and the fishes. How exciting to be part of this grand and divine plan to foster more love and kindness in our world.

It might be that there are only one or two Fairy Godmothers and Beary Godfathers in a neighborhood who are disguised as ordinary men and women. For certain, they are out there in the world responding to opportunities to share, care, love and generate kindness because there are so many opportunities and lots of loving seeds to be planted. There is enough for all of us to do, and be, just like the lyrics, "do-be do-be do" made popular by Frank Sinatra and the song *Strangers in the Night* . . . What a sweet way to go through life, don't you think?

Our affirmation for this chapter:
I am always in the right place at the right time with an open heart.

Questions to deepen your awareness:
1. Was there ever an opportunity to follow your heart instead of your daily planner and what happened?
2. Can you remember an experience where you did something beautiful or kind for no apparent reason?
3. Have you ever had a synchronistic event that changed your mind or attitude for the better?
4. Write about a synchronistic event that happened to you, if you don't have one, write about someone else's or make one up.

Chapter 6

Y ~ You Saying "Yes" to Love

"Love is the opening door, love is what we came here for,
no one could offer you more, do you know what I mean,
have your eyes really seen. . . ."

~ BERNIE TAUPIN FROM "LOVE SONG"

Finally, the Fairy Godmother's goal is to say "yes" to love, wherever it leads her. We're talking about universal, divine love that transcends gender, race, religion or circumstance and the surrender to the power of "unconditional loving" for oneself and for others. This is how "you" the embodiment of Divine Mothering, i.e., the Fairy Godmother manifests itself in the world and transforms it.

All together this could be an overwhelming project, but by taking one step and one moment at a time, I believe it is possible. The more we consciously make unconditional love our intention, the more it becomes a habit and then we are able to respond to life in a more loving compassionate way, love is the open door so what are we waiting for?

I believe that love is an action word and by taking action with heartfelt expression, whether it is a silent prayer, performing a helpful task, or an act of kindness or courage, we are fulfilling it. Love can nurture, protect, sustain, connect us to others and most of all, love can heal because the lack of love is usually at the core of our wounds. So, this is a time to rise above it and come into the full potential of loving, within ourselves and our world.

One of the more unique circumstances that bears out this truth is that love is demonstrated through the phenomena of NDE's (Near Death Experiences). My sister, for example, gave me the gift of her love at a very critical time in her life, which was touching, heart-warming, almost "angelic" and gave me a feeling of connection with her, which ultimately recalibrated our relationship.

She had a terrible car accident and was thrown 80 feet through the windshield of her car. When she finally gained consciousness and surgeons put her head back together, we talked. She shared her experience that she traveled through a passageway where there was a great light at the end. When she arrived at the opening of that light, she was greeted by luminous beings whose energy and light gave her a rich and deep feeling of love. They asked her, "Is there any reason for you to stay?" My sister didn't want to leave her two daughters alone. She was then asked, "Is there anyone you need to express love to?" She couldn't remember how she answered that question. It's a fact that when people have these NDE's (Near Death Experiences), they seldom reflect on their worldly possessions, yet often think of what they wanted to do with their lives, who they loved and were leaving behind. We have a chance as Fairy Godmothers to make a difference in our world, to expand our capacity to love and experience fulfillment and that's exciting to me.

This is a primary example of the importance of love in our lives. Love is important to the very fiber of life. Love is the golden thread that weaves our lives together. When the chips are down and there's nowhere to go, it isn't the Cadillac we own, or the boat we possess that makes us happy. It is the people in our lives that are "family" to us, the connection we make with the universe, and our need to communicate our love to each other. Love has the ability to tie up the loose ends hanging from of our tapestry called humanity.

Merriam-Webster dictionary says that, "*love is a feeling of warm personal attachment or deep affection for a friend, parent or child,*" and I find truth in that. What I have concluded about loving God (or higher power) is that it is objective, neutral, and cherishing by nature. The great mystical texts of all religions talks about the essence and love of God existing in every soul, in every human being. It is available to us in many other ways, but primarily through each other and through our personal relationship with ourselves and the Divine.

As we try to weave the thread of love through the ups and downs of our life tapestry, it is to me, a soulful task. Like the song says, "Love is what we came here for, who could offer you more". I feel the essence of love is needed more now than ever before. There are places and circumstances where there still isn't enough love in our families, our world, etc. One of our greatest teachers of love, Jesus the Christ, said per 1 John 4:8 KVJ, "God is love." As a Fairy Godmother I continue to see more lovers of humanity in everyday life and yet there is more of the healing and nourishing presence of love needed.

Fairy Godmothers, our intention and vision is to foster more love within ourselves and to share it with others. Whatever the circumstances, I am holding, and I hope you agree, to see and create more love in your world now, in our lifetime. We do this, moment by moment and one person at a time by choosing love.

In our educational system, the idea of self-love is relegated to our churches, psychology, self-help books and inspirational texts. Now its life-giving message is coming to us via TV and the Internet by great thinkers, lovers of humanity, and inspirational speakers such as Depok Chopra, Oprah Winfree, Ekhart Tolle, and more. While they are making progress, we are still experiencing an increase in drug abuse and teen pregnancies. More work in the trenches, more self-love, love of others, and comradery is needed for the greater good.

That requires us to let go of our ideas of separateness and embrace the ideas of the unifying effects of loving kindness and compassion, the real value in our everyday life.

My story of separateness began at home between the ages of 2 and 13 years. I was raised in a dangerous area of Los Angeles. The idea of community was non-existent. I didn't grow up with a sense of community or sense of belonging. The world "out there" was scary and sometimes down-right dangerous. In my world, my family was lacking in the expression of love. For me, love of animals, nature, art and music was my personal journey and the replacement for what I didn't have. Then there was the love for God, which I learned about in Sunday school, but which I had an inner knowing that God did exist. I loved my mom, dad and sister, but it wasn't reciprocated. It was as if no one knew how to express their love. Without a role model, I never learned how to express my feelings very well. As time went on, I built up a wall of defensiveness to protect myself from the pain of not having loving experiences.

This is when I received a calling, which would become my purpose in life. The emotional pain I experienced became the greatest wound in my life. I had no gold thread to weave into my tapestry, so, in the beginning, I started to look for it in all the wrong places. I realized there was a big hole in my life experience that I didn't quite understand. Love was an elusive quality that never seemed to come my way. I would eventually meet a spiritual teacher who helped me to really understand love and it started with me learning to love myself.

In the interim, I felt vulnerable and experienced feelings of helplessness and hopelessness and found it increasingly difficult to overcome the emotional barrier that I'd built for myself. The wall represented security to me. I was unwilling or unable to accept love for fear of feeling more unworthy, inadequate, and unloved. Fear is a difficult thing to reign in. It can penetrate your subconscious and work its nasty tendrils into your psyche and consume you with dread and anxiety. Sometimes, it's just hanging back from a loving expression that is coming your way and because you are shy and fear risking rejection you find yourself hanging back as though no one would really want to hug you. The risk exists even when someone you know offers friendship. Who do you trust when you can't trust yourself?

Those of us who have had the blessings of a spiritual guide as I have, know if we can diffuse our separateness, we might be able to surrender to love. Surrendering to loving myself was a huge insurmountable obstacle since I had no idea where to begin. Working with my mentor gave me some ideas to begin the process. I believe that the truly great spiritual teachers of all times were teachers of love and inner peace.

Sometimes the greatest hurdle to having more love can be not knowing how to express it for fear of rejection. My even greater fear, which became a learned response, was fear of losing it. Our true nature is synonymous with our Creator who gives us life and also gives us *love*. I am by no means the expert on the essence of how to love. I'm still learning, but I am seeking and working every day to express more and receive more love. I find inspiration in the wisdom of another lover of humanity:

> *"Your task is not to seek for love, but merely to seek and find*
> *all the barriers within yourself that you have built against it."*
>
> ~ RUMI

As we connect with our inner being, the "treasures outside of us" can't compare with the treasures that we can find within ourselves. Whatever you do, do it with love.

Here is a meditation that helps me connect to the love that I am:

- Take a few moments for yourself now (at least 10–20 minutes). Find a quiet place to sit, back supported, feet on the floor. The place that works for me is in my backyard under the trees or in my meditation chair in my office. Your place could be a place in nature, a garden or in a quiet room. The idea is to be in a quiet place where you won't be disturbed and you could put a "do not disturb" sign on the door.
- Close your eyes. Take a few deep cleansing breaths, breathing in through your nose deep into your belly and out through your slightly parted lips; 3–5 times is enough.
- Now tap your heart lightly. Focus again on your breathing. Envision that your breath is coming into your heart center and that you are breathing in and out through your heart center.
- Now that you are in this centered, heartfelt place, think of someone you love. It could be your partner, your child, your pet, spiritual teacher, etc.

If you can't think of someone, go to a place you love, perhaps in nature, with trees, flowers. Go in your imagination to whomever or wherever you have a feeling of deep love for.

- Continue breathing in and out of your heart focusing on your loved one or loving experience so that you're breathing the love that is present into yourself. Let your feelings of love flow in and out through your heart center.

- Now allow your heart breath with that beautiful feeling of love rise from your heart up into your head, calming and soothing your mind. Then through your imagination, send it out the top of your head as light. It could be pink or gold, violet, or iridescent white. Allow this breath of light filled with your love to come back down and enter you through the front of your body back into your heart. Continue this heart breath for at least 5 times.

- Finally, just drift on this loving energy that is "your very own love." This can be a great time to repeat an affirmation of self-love. I find that floating sense of spiritual love and my own heart energy extremely nourishing. It's also helpful in times of stress after some physical exercise or movement and/or free form writing. I find this meditation liberating because it helps me to move beyond any upset or separation that I might be experiencing.

Another way we can say yes to love is to offer a hug. Our society historically has become more physically reserved and it's time to change that. There have been many university studies that show that we need at least eight hugs per day for healthy living. Hugs lower blood pressure, increase oxytocin levels (feel good hormones), heals loneliness, anger, isolation, depression, etc. Longer hugs lift our serotonin levels, elevate moods and create happiness. They can relax muscles, take away pain, soothe aches by increasing circulation into the soft tissue, and can balance out our nervous system. Children who are hugged frequently are less anxious adults because hugs connect us to our ability to love ourselves.

The essence of love lives within each one of us and is available if we just stop for a moment and look within ourselves to connect to it. So, now I invite you to come along on this journey, this adventure of love, with me. There are so many people and places in the world that need it.

Our affirmation for this chapter:
I am a clear and an open channel for God's healing love.

Questions to deepen your awareness:
1. Can I allow myself to give and receive eight hugs today? Who will I hug?
2. Do I know an older person who is alone a lot, will I go and give them a hug or two?
3. Remember an experience of love I had as a child, as an adult, and write about it in my journal.
4. Where in my life can I reach out to give or receive more love? What does that look like?

Chapter 7

Are You Fairy Godmother Material?

"The more you are motivated by love,
the more fearless and free your action will be"

~ DALAI LAMA

As we begin our journey into creating a more loving, kind, gentle world we have to look closely at what we are committing to. Yes, commitment is a strong word, but if we are to become the force for the good that we are capable of, which we want, we will have to commit. Commitment isn't a loose term, but something that once we set it in motion, like intention, it is a creative force within itself and within ourselves. Without it we cannot hope to be the power of love in this world and, indeed, this is what being a Fairy Godmother and Beary Godfather is about. The commitment I ask of you and you should ask yourself is "Can you sort through your life using the lens of loving kindness and compassion in order to see through the eyes of a Fairy Godmother?" If so, then you can start the process of grounding yourself in actual activities of inner and outer alignment.

So here are some questions to test whether you have the "right stuff" or should I say the "loving stuffing" to give the magical, miraculous love of a Fairy Godmother into the world. They are:

1. Do you have some time in your life to share with others? As you go through your day, are you willing to perform one act of kindness every day?
2. Do you have an "empty nest" or an empty schedule and an open heart you can share with others?
3. Are you open to learning more about love and loving?
4. Are you willing to give and receive love as kindness, caring, and compassion in ordinary encounters and extraordinary moments of heartfelt sharing?

5. Are you willing to believe in the power of love and want more peace in the world?

6. Are you good at being flexible and willing to learn how to remain neutral, taking nothing personally and letting go of "against-ness" in order to make a place for more peace inside yourself and our world?

7. Are you willing to take care of yourself so you can help take care of others?

8. Are you willing to cultivate the habit of asking God for Light, inner guidance and peace and to listen within to your still small voice of intuition? Can you make time to listen to God for answers by meditating and praying for at least 15 minutes to an hour each day?

If you answered "yes" to at least three or more questions then you are Fairy Godmother/Beary Godfather material.

Take a few moments now and write down which of the above most resonates in your heart. Choose which aspects really call out to you and write about it in your journal. You can even write down scenarios of you "doing" an act of kindness, any ideas of where to start, where you might have seen a circumstance already waiting for your warmth and kindness. I suggest you create a journal that has only Fairy Godmother entries in it and vow to write in it every day even if it's only a sentence or two.

Next, look at the items that you think or feel are more than you can do. Remember, all can be learned and practiced and you might surprise yourself as you begin your journey as a Fairy Godmother at how quickly you evolve, how fulfilling and how much more fun and interesting your life will become.

Remember, you can go about your life on the surface pretty much as usual except for special Fairy Godmother projects, the commitment to doing at least one act of kindness each day and meditating or praying for 15 minutes to an hour. As you start to implement these activities into your daily routine it will be your new inner insight that may be the biggest shift, and that occurs in your attitude and a more expanded outlook on life. Like the ability to see other people in the world who are different than you, as a beautiful kaleidoscope of diversity in color, food, language, etc., instead of setting them apart from you. Seeing through the eyes of a Fairy Godmother means you realize that all people have families, experience tragedies, have children they worry about, dreams they want to fulfill just like we do. They might even want to join us in service as the Fairy Godmothers* in their communities.

Benefits of Becoming a Fairy Godmother

1. Not only will the world become a sweeter and safer place, but you will learn the art of self-love for we cannot give what we do not have.
2. Scientific studies have proven that serotonin, a biochemical in the body is increased when we perform acts of kindness. Serotonin increases the feelings of joy and well-being in the body and the emotions. It also increases the body's immune system and here's the kicker! It enhances the one receiving the act of kindness, and the one who gives through the act of kindness and it even does the same for those who only observe an act of kindness being expressed. Now if that is not a good enough reason, better health and happiness, yeah!
3. We can benefit from the inner peace we are creating, which results in better sleep by taking better care of ourselves emotionally and physically.
4. As we create greater inner peace within ourselves, we create it in the world. The new science of Quantum Physics has proven that as more and more people are peaceful within themselves and hold more loving kindness in their minds and emotions more of it is created in the world, as a whole, beginning with our own homes, communities, and in the world. I don't know about you, but I sleep better knowing that more peace and kindness is taking over the world at large because I and others like me are creating it, daily.
5. Instead of getting caught up in the daily news of global and community chaos and violence, etc. and becoming depressed about it, we can reside in the knowingness that ours is a voice and an action for peace. Through our work of placing situations and circumstances globally in the light of God, sending thoughts enhanced by feelings of peace and prosperity out to those troubled places, we no longer sit there feeling helpless, hopeless or depressed about the state of the world. We can live in more positivity and the sheer joy that we are making a difference.
6. We become part of the solution and not contributors to the problems by refraining from doom and gloom thoughts. We not only enhance the possibilities for more good in the world, but we are actually holding space for it. We can relax in the knowing that through our intention as a Fairy Godmother we are creating it. We then have feelings of making a difference, of confidence in the power of love that we are, of feeling powerful not powerless. We are contributing to the good of the world and part of the transformation of our lives, our communities, our world, regardless of our physical or financial situation.

   If we have the money and the physical abilities, we can help in these cases, but if we don't, no matter who or where we are, we make a difference. We are creating a more gentle, kind and peaceful world and again we can sleep better knowing it is becoming a reality. We need to know that and act as if it is true until the transformation becomes the "rule of the day" instead of the opposite downward spiral.

Finally, there is a nourishing of the Soul that takes place as we prepare to bring more love into the world. As we connect to our own inner Beloved, we bring even more love into our world. It cannot be otherwise. In reading Eckhart Tolle's book, "The Power of Now," I learned that as we remain in our center, in the present moment, the now, the anger and crazy making thoughts and feelings have no place to go. They dissolve and what we are left with is the Beloved and its glorious peace and from that peace we are washed with the love of our soul, our true self. No judgment, no past, no future, just the glorious peace of the here and now and that is some of the most powerful magic we have, the magic of divine love for ourselves first so we can share from our overflow.

So for the love of the world, we are taught to love ourselves, to give from our overflow. If you are truly Fairy Godmother material, this is a no brainer. What do you have to lose? An angry, chaotic world? Feelings of powerlessness and depression? A lack of joy and sense of purpose?

Fairy Godmothers and Beary Godfathers come in many shapes and sizes. They show themselves in the form of caring teachers that see a child's potential and continues to encourage. They come in the form of grandparents who take children for walks in the park or take their service dog to the library or to shut-ins. They may be very young and want to help the elderly by taking out the trash without being asked. My own great granddaughter, Traci, always befriends the kids that don't fit in on the playground at lunch or recess. If there are bullies, she stays with the targeted child to protect and befriend him/her. She also is very gentle and patient with younger children. What kind of a Fairy Godmother will you be?

Here is a well-known story I found that bears repeating because it demonstrates the power we have at any given moment in time. I changed the main character from a man to a woman. . . . being partial to Fairy Godmothers. It's called the Starfish Story.

The Starfish Story

Once upon a time, there was a wise man who used to go to the ocean to do his writing. He had a habit of walking on the beach before he began his work.

One day, as he was walking along the shore, he looked down the beach and saw a human figure moving like a dancer. He smiled to himself at the thought of someone who would dance to the day, and so, he walked faster to catch up.

As he got closer, he noticed that the figure was that of a young woman, and that what she was doing was not dancing at all. The young woman was reaching down to the shore, picking up small objects, and throwing them into the ocean.

He came closer still and called out "Good morning! What you are doing?"

The young woman looked up, and replied "Throwing starfish into the ocean."

"Why are you throwing starfish into the ocean?" asked the somewhat startled wise man.

To this, the young woman replied, "The sun is up and the tide is going out. If I don't throw them in, they'll die."

Upon hearing this, the wise man commented, "But, young woman, have you not seen that there are miles and miles of beach and there are starfish all along every mile? You can't possibly make a difference!"

At this, the young woman bent down, picked up another starfish, and threw it into the ocean. As it met the water, she said, "It made a difference for that one." At this point, the wise man abandoned his writing and spent the morning throwing starfish back into the ocean.

~ Original story by Loren Eisely, *The Immense Journey*

Our affirmation for this chapter:
I am the love of Spirit, joyfully expressing my love wherever I am.

Questions to deepen your awareness:
1. How will your life change as you become the Fairy Godmother?
2. What habits do you have that will support you?
3. What expressions will you be giving up?
4. How will you celebrate your good works?
5. Who can you share your wins with?

Chapter 8

From a World without Love to a Life of Healing and Purpose

*"No matter how your heart is grieving, if you keep on believing,
the dreams that you wish will come true."*

~ WALT DISNEY

Once upon a time there was a little baby girl of questionable parentage who was left in a basket at a railroad watering tower in the late 1800's near Star Valley, Wyoming, with the hope she would be given a home and would survive. This was my mother's mother.

We all start somewhere in life. Usually our first encounters in childhood are with our parents and their attitudes, values, economic circumstances, emotional maturity, communication skills, etc. Then we have extended family, religious and societal influences that affect the decisions we make growing up that in turn can affect us our whole life through. Not all people have complicated beginnings, and God bless them and theirs, for me and mine that was not to be.

Depending on those early factors, we can live with a positive intent, believing in the good, hoping for the best outcomes, making positive choices and thereby create accordingly. But if we take the downward path, the path of negative thoughts and feelings, fearfulness, making poor choices in how we see and deal with life, we have very different outcomes. In the end, we either rise like the phoenix out of the ashes or we sink into a pattern of resignation to a life of struggle, limitation and lack.

My relationship with the "Fairy Godmother" was born from my struggles in early life and my desire and vision for something better. I didn't want anyone to feel the loneliness and sadness I felt so often in my childhood. I decided I wanted more love in the world, not just for myself, but for everyone, everywhere. I became the Godchild in search of a Fairy Godmother.

I am a third generation un-mothered child and have spent not only my childhood but most my adult life searching for love "in all the wrong places". . . . it would seem. Because the kind of loving I needed, desperately I might add, was nowhere to be found.

A mother's love is instinctive unless there has been a deep wounding. I believe that my mother had love for me as an instinct but based on my childhood experience, she was unable to express that love. You cannot share very successfully a quality that you have not learned or experienced. The lack of loving experiences, my mother's, her mother's and mine, became the inability to share the love we were wanting and needing with our own family and so has been perpetuated to some degree onto our fourth and fifth generations, my grandchildren and great grandchildren.

As a child I found that feeling love and expressing love were two different things. I needed to have the expression of love physically, through touching, and I didn't get that. As a child like all children, I had to desperately believe that my parents loved me. It's built into a child to see their parent as a kind of God in their life that provides for their very existence, i.e. food, shelter, and in most cases touching, nurturing, protecting, etc.

I also know that I loved my children very much. In fact, most of their childhood, my life revolved around them and their needs, but it was more of a dutiful caring, not so much of an emotionally nurturing care. This is partly due to being a single parent most of their childhoods, exhausted at the end of my work day, no down time, just dinner, shopping, laundry, and I just fell into bed. Then came the teen years, bickering, etc. To make matters worse, I was also totally ignorant of what an emotionally nurturing parent or spouse looked like. I was married three times to addicts and alcoholics because I didn't know better, didn't love or take care of myself. My only positive models were in movies.

My story is how I came from what felt like a loveless life into finding my own love inside myself and having a deep sense of purpose toward creating more real love in the world. My learning and my salvation has been connecting to the love within, the Beloved, and wanting to share the awareness of the power of that love to heal and transform lives on a personal and global scale. I know I am not the only one. It's everywhere, and in these later days, especially since the 60's, the acceptance of the power of love like the song says . . . *"is in the air."*

My grandmother was found and raised by a family who named her Laura. As she grew up, not being part of the natural family, she had less than ideal self-esteem. She met and married a hardworking, well-meaning man named Bill who fostered a stern attitude toward family and child raising. He himself was one of thirteen children who came to live in America by entering through a cow pasture gate from Canada, and migrating to the Wyoming territory which later became the heart of the "dust bowl" in the 1930's.

Laura gave birth to five children at a very young age herself, three girls and twin boys. Because of the extreme economic conditions Bill had to be away from home for weeks at a time, working on the railroad, punching cows, breaking horses, doing whatever he could to keep a roof over their head, and food on the table. Whether through loneliness or restlessness, Laura lapsed into alcoholism. One day Bill came home to someone else in their bed and he beat the man almost to death. Grandpa Bill was well respected and although his actions were understood, the Sheriff said that if he didn't leave for a while, he'd have to take him in and he'd probably wind up serving jail time so he left, always sending money to the family. When all the talk died down and he made his way back home, it was to an empty house. He found out from the neighbors that Laura had taken the children to the outlying State run homes, orphanages and left them there.

Bill went from orphanage to orphanage and collected all his children. He connected with his own parents, older by now, and they set up housekeeping in an austere two story house in Wyoming surrounded by the ravages of drought. The dust bowl offered little employment and it took all of them to just keep the house. One of Laura's children, a tiny waif of a girl, was my mother Ruby. She was very small and had contracted Rheumatic fever at a very young age and almost died. She only went to school till the 6th grade and only grew to be 4 feet 9 inches tall.

Ruby never talked much about her early beginnings, but if ever there was a child in need of a fairy Godmother, or grandparents who could stay home with her as a child, it was Ruby. No one really knows what happened at the orphanage but she never fully recovered from her childhood emotionally.

There were only a few stories that I remember mom telling from her childhood. She was very proud and very private. The one that helped me understand her most was the one memory she had of her mother coming to visit once when she was maybe six years old. On this particular day, a car pulled up and a thin, small woman got out. As she was walking up the stairs, both girls were waiting on the porch to see her. Laura looked at Ruby's sister Viona, went to her, kissing and hugging her. Bill finally said "Laura, here's Ruby" she just looked up and waved, but never left Viona's side. The mother came and went, never so much as speaking to Ruby. As long as I knew my mother, even up to the day she died, she refused to acknowledge that she had a mother. I ask, "Where was her Fairy Godmother"?

This inability to connect to a child was to revisit a second generation. As I grew up, I was often left to my own devices out in the yard where I bonded with nature, the birds and animals of the yard, and especially the trees. Mom was in the house with my little sister, again there was a bonding with one child and not the other. I would be sent outdoors and called back in when it was time to fix dinner, mom didn't cook either, she just told me what to do and I cooked and I'd better be done before my father came home.

My only saving grace in these times was that I felt quite "at home" with the land. We lived on two city lots, filled with trees, lawns and rose bushes of my grandmother's. I would gather flowers and make little stone circles, placing them in the circle, under the trees. When I did that, I noticed the birds would come closer and sit near me so they became my friends, I loved their cheerful little voices singing their little songs. I talked to my favorite tree, and it was during these moments I poured my heart out to the world of nature. I told the tree, birds, all who might be listening, how much I wanted to have a real friend, someone to talk to and how lonely I was. Mother Nature was and has always been there for me. Many times I took refuge in the wild places, the mountains, the forests. I was always able to find myself in this way, which lead me to studying the Medicine Wheel teachings later on in my life. I actually spent six years going from spiritual camp to camp learning from Native American elders, how to live in balance with myself and the Earth Mother.

I also talked to Mary, the mother of Jesus, because at Sunday school I was told that she was the mother of compassion that listened to the prayers of those who were hurt and sad. She was always there for me, out in the yard. When I was disciplined I would run outside and hide among the trees. To this day, I feel that being in the wild places in nature is sacred. They are cathedrals of the mother earth. I remember feeling so sad at times that I would lay down on the grass under my favorite tree and cry myself to sleep.

I was born with a cleft pallet, which caused considerable problems in my early life, and I was not able to take in nourishment. I know it must have been very frustrating for my very young mother and I was extremely dairy intolerant. Finally, they found that canned goat's milk created the least mucus.

As I grew older and tried to talk, I was not able to be understood very well. People said I talked like I had a mouth full of mush. Although I was operated on when I was only a few days old it was still a huge problem. Because I almost died at childbirth, I was kept in the hospital and not able to go home with my mother. In the first few months of an infant's life, the mother bonds with their child, a natural occurrence. I didn't go home until I was about 6 weeks old. Later, a hip joint deformity was discovered so I had to use crutches for a few years between six and eight years old.

I am sure my entrance into my mother's life was fraught with disappointment. Since my beginning was so difficult, it was no wonder I felt, from early on, that I didn't belong, and worse, I also felt I must have done something to drive them away. All this probably lead to my very low self-esteem. As time went on and no closeness grew, I was sure that I was a burden and so I grew up without a sense of belonging. The household was also a "spare the rod, spoil the child" and I still carry the emotional as well as physical scars.

Another one of the stories I remember my mom telling me, was from when she went to school. She said that they had so little food in the house that most often she did not even have a lunch to take to school. She would get up and come down the stairs, about half way down she could see out the window from the stairs, and as far as the eye could see there was only dirt, no green of fields, no trees, just dirt, dust devils, and flat, hot, open land.

She would come down stairs into the kitchen, and if she was lucky there was a pot of black strong coffee on the stove. She would pour herself a cup of coffee and then go off to walk to school. She said that if she was very lucky they had bread and onions which she made into an onion sandwich, but most the time she didn't have anything to eat until dinner when they all came together to eat their one meal a day. Her grandmother, who was off working mostly and who she didn't remember much of, would take flour sacks and make a plain shift dress for her since she was so small. Flour in those days came in these cotton bags with string sewing them together at the top and they had flower prints on them, and that was the only dress she remembers. This was such an austere beginning. No one had time for her and she was rather sickly her whole life and she felt small. Where was her Fairy Godmother?

We were very poor as I grew up. We lived in a very old, small, two bedroom shack-like house that was located behind my paternal grandmother's grand two story house. Our house was older than the big house. It was like a servants quarters really.

We lived in a very dangerous part of town, two blocks from where the Watts race riots occurred, a few years after we moved. Given this, we were not allowed to play with anyone in the neighborhood. We were the only white children to go to this school and I was routinely followed home with catcalls and rocks thrown at me, etc. You get the picture.

My mom had only two friends. One of them was a kindly older Irish woman named Anna. She lived about two miles away and would take the bus down to our street and come to visit my mom. Anna always had a smile on her face, and an Irish twinkle in her eye. She had a great sense of humor and was always finding something to laugh about, the most cheerful and kindest woman I knew as a child. She always had a little time to connect with me. I instinctively knew that Anna got who I was and looked past my "disabilities" into my innocent little heart. I don't remember ever being looked at with a sense of innocence by my mother but it was always there in Anna.

One day Anna came to visit and I wanted to see her. They were in the house by the front door. I banged on the screen door. I could hear them talking but no one responded to my cries and my pounding. So I quietly sat there on the porch just soaking up the girl talk. At one point, Anna said to my mom "Diana looks just like Fred (my father)". My mom quickly replied . . . "yea, poor thing". I think I was about 6 years old and I knew right then (or thought I did) that my mom didn't like me because I was ugly, apparently, like my dad . . . children don't judge their parents in terms of pretty or ugly, they are just our mom and dad. At that tender age of six I interpreted this all to mean that I was ugly, deformed and didn't fit in, even with my own family and that decision would color my whole life.

I do believe that Anna was the only experience of a real live Fairy Godmother I ever had in my young life, other than the Disney movies, oh and my kindergarten teacher. I spent other brief moments with Anna when she occasionally baby sat me. I guess my sister was with my parents. I treasured these times. I always felt that she saw me for who I was, not what my mother was afraid I was. I have felt Anna's presence in still quiet moments and I can still see her smiling Irish eyes. I have had Psychics describe her and tell me that she's still with me, like a guardian angel or a "Fairy Godmother". In some ways, Anna befriending my mom, served as a kind of Fairy Godmother to my mother also. Here was just one well-meaning, loving, simple, caring person who, whether she knew it or not, changed lives just by sharing herself with others.

"Life itself is the most wonderful fairy tale."

~ HANS CHRISTIAN ANDERSON

My grandmothers are both long time gone, and so are my mother and father. I wasn't able to bring much solace or fairy magic to them and their lives, but the changes I've made in viewing my life and my childhood have led to a very important aspect of generational healing, and that is forgiveness. In the Cherokee tradition of the white crystal medicine that I was fortunate enough to learn about, a person's work on themselves and the healing of their wounds and their dysfunction is extended back in time seven generations and also extended forward for seven generations. So given this amazing spiritual promise, how could we ignore it? It is another one of spirit's demonstrations of the power of love.

Because I have been able to come to a different understanding and forgiveness of my childhood wounds, abandonments and sadness I can now reshape my own next generation's lives, and it all started with forgiveness, acceptance and the belief in the power of love.

Whether I believed in love blindly because it was a desperate need in me or it arose when I began a spiritual journey, the outcome is the same. I looked for love, never gave up, and in the end I found it. Now I want to share it, spread the good news about the power of love, and how to heal ourselves with it and heal our world.

"You have to keep breaking your heart until it opens."

~ RUMI

For me, the journey to be loved and to find love has been like setting myself up for heartbreak but another way to look at it is that the break in our heart is the crack through which the Light can come.

In the Bible I John 4:8, it says, "God is love". Another reference I found was that our inner love, love for ourselves and God's love has been spoken and written about as the Beloved, that we can embrace ourselves as the Beloved. In my prayers I refer to God as "Beloved of my Soul". Our soul being that part of us that is the spark of God within. I cannot write a book about love and leave God out of it can I? Whatever God is to you, whatever name you call God, whatever vision or feeling you have of your higher power, the story is about your relationship to God and love.

In Joseph Campbell's *"Hero with a Thousand Faces"*, the Hero starts out by experiencing a wounding and leaves his home and family. On his journey he encounters a guide or mentor that may take an animal or human form. He does battle of some kind and must go "underground", as in the unconscious or dream state, an otherworldly place where he must confront an unwanted part of himself. He must defeat the monster he finds there, and through that victory he experiences a change in his own awareness and receives a prize or a treasure. At the end of the story he returns home wiser and better able to love his home and shares the bounty of his treasure with his community.

"Our life evokes our character. You find out more about
yourself as you go on. That's why it is good to be able to
put yourself in situations that will evoke your higher nature."

~ JOSEPH CAMPBELL, THE POWER OF MYTH

As in the Hero's Journey, all of us who believe . . . in love and in Fairy Godmothers . . . are heroes who have the power to bring more love into our world. Each person expressing love through acts of kindness, caring, sharing and the sending of Light into our world, healing the dark places, healing the wounds in themselves and their communities through service, is setting love in motion. It is the sharing of our love with our world, right here, right now, that bridges the gap of chaos, separation and the resulting violence in our world. This occurs one person, one community, one country at a time. We will have Fairy Godmothers and Beary Godfathers everywhere in the world.

> *"When you bring yourself into a loving consciousness with all things, peace and harmony will enfold your heart, and you will recognize within every level of your being-ness that there is only love."*
>
> ~ JOHN-ROGER, DSS, LOVING EACH DAY

Yes, many of us have suffered childhood wounds as well as the loss of loved ones, finances, homes, etc. but are we going to let the wounding define us and our world? There has been far too much of that down through time.

Our wounds are our power in disguise. When a seed is planted in fertile ground, it has to push its way up to the surface and break through to the sun. Being held "under" the earth as it heats up, in spring, gives it strength to grow. If it doesn't grow strong enough to "push through", it will never make it through the wind and the rain and the sun beating down. It will be too weak, never become what it was meant to be.

We were not created to fail, or to have everything "easy" in life. Why? Because we would not grow in our character, our strength, our ability to love. In the end, it's love that matters. It's love that we take with us, not the money, not the Cadillac, not the jewelry, etc. I believe life is like a kind of graduate school. We come here to grow in all ways possible, emotionally, mentally, physically and spiritually. No path that is worth walking is easy, but it is strength-building at its most complete. We cannot leave compassion and kindness out of it.

> *"You, of all people, deserve a happy ending despite everything that has happened to you. You aren't bitter, you aren't cold, you've just retreated a little and been shy, and that's okay. If I were a fairy godmother, I would give you your heart's desire in an instant and I would wipe away your tears and tell you not to cry. . . ."*
>
> ~ SYLVAIN REYNARD, GABRIEL'S INFERNO

I encourage you to find as in the hero's journey, your inner treasure. And sometimes our mentors are our strengths as we grow into them, learning how to use them to navigate our way to the fulfilment of our quest.

My quest is to love myself and share my love from the overflow. To create a kinder, gentler, more loving world for myself and my family and for all future generations. Yes, we will have obstacles to overcome. We will have tears of sadness and tears of joy, but we won't be doing it all by ourselves, alone. There will be Fairy Godmothers and Beary Godfathers to turn to along the way, to ask "which way to the Land of Oz?" Helpers to encourage us and appreciate us. Let's get on with discovering our Fairy Godmother tools, so we can be prepared.

With the message I received as a child, that I was ugly, a burden and didn't belong, this is the affirmation for this chapter that has helped me, I hope it inspires you also.

Our affirmation for this chapter:
"I am the love of Spirit, trusting my open heart, flowing with peace, beauty and joy"

Some questions to ponder:
1. What inspires you to be strong?
2. What gave you hope during times of grief, abandonment, loss?
3. Was there someone in your life that was a fairy godmother to you? Write about your experience.
4. What are the ways you express love to the people in your life?
5. Did you or do you still have a spirit guide, animal-helper or angel?

Chapter 9

Tools for Today's Fairy Godmother

"All the world is made of faith, and trust, and pixie dust."

~ James M. Barrie

Although, we will be working with fairy dust and not pixie dust, some of the working tools of Fairy Godmothers are legendary such as her magic words and her magic wand. Here we will also be examining some of the not-so-famous tools, but just the same, make no mistake, they are extremely important.

One of these was her ability to **magically appear at the perfect moment** when she was needed. Glinda the good witch traveled in a giant bubble. Dorothy had her magic with her the whole time, her ruby red slippers, but only after learning about her strengths and gaining courage through her trials was the power revealed to her.

As we set our intention to be guided intuitively to where we can do the most good on any given day, we will, magically show up just in time, in the perfect place and know exactly what is needed. Our wisdom from living life will inform us and our loving heart will guide us.

So, set your intention, be conscious that you are transforming the world, little by little, wherever you find yourself, daily, momentarily. When you wonder what you can do, ask and then listen. Be aware and look for the good and kind things you can do all around you. Believe me, you will receive the assistance and guidance that you need. Remember what happened to Tinkerbell? Captain Hook poisoned her. While she lay dying, Peter Pan asked the audience to tell Tinkerbell that they believed in her and then she came back. Her light began to shine, the darkness shrank away, and all was in harmony once again.

Fairy Godmothers also had a kind of alchemical knowledge of how to **change the form of things.** Most of the time, she didn't pull them out of thin air. She transformed what was present in the environment or what she found in a person. She also had the ability to see what was needed and to elicit assistance from whomever and wherever. She lived in the magical world, so she still had to abide by its rules, making bargains, exchanges, honoring boundaries, etc. There was always a price to pay hence, Cinderella had to come home at the "strike" of midnight. Sleeping Beauty did not die, but fell into a deep sleep along with her whole family and community until the day she was awakened by her true love's kiss. Shrek's Fiona was an earthly girl by day, but an ogre by night. As it turned out, her true love Shrek, matched her true form, which she herself chose.

How do we change the form of things? We change our attitudes, we try to see things from an expanded perspective, in other words, see the bigger picture. With our tools of kindness, open mindedness, and willingness, we will do this, too. The "trade-offs" or transformation we can make can be trading thoughts of fear that create separation for acceptance and positivity, a good word and a smile for defensiveness, and finally, embracing the good in ourselves and others to meet fear with Light and Love. People want to be seen and heard. They want the benefit of the doubt. This is how we Fairy Godmothers can change the form of things. Oh, a little creative gifting can also work miracles. Here's one of my stories for *changing the form of things—* a day in my life as a Fairy Godmother.

I was at a local store one day. When I came out, I saw a young man in his early twenties sitting outside with his dog. He was so thin, eyes cast downward, not really asking for anything, just sitting there as if to say, "What now?" I was going to get dog food at my next stop so I asked him if he had food for his dog. He looked a little startled that I even spoke to him. He answered "no, not really." So, I offered to get food for his friend, the dog. He tucked his head into his chest, looked down and said that he didn't want to be a bother. I explained that I have dogs and suggested that we get our dogs some food. He shared his name as well as his dog's name. I purchased a 4 lb. bag for him since he was on foot couldn't carry too much weight around. We then stopped at a drive through hamburger place where I bought food for both of us. We ate our burgers and shared tidbits about our dogs and ourselves. I then asked him if I could drop him some-where and he told me no. I wished him and his dog the best and added, "God bless you on your journey." I bid them both farewell and I never saw him again. What I did see was the love and care he had for his dog and that was enough for me. It probably cost me a total of $15 to feed us all and for a small price I know I made the difference for him that day. Maybe, I even encouraged him to go home or at least believe in the goodness of people. I transformed two lives that day, his and mine because I went home very happy and spiritually nourished, a rather priceless experience for me.

The more well-known accoutrements of a Fairy Godmother are her **magic wand** and her **magic words.** The tools for our work in today's world are a little different, but make no mistake, the magic is just as powerful for us as it was in the world of myth and fantasy. The reason fairy tales and mythology have stayed with us is their impact on our deeper psyche. They are somewhat of a road map of awareness.

What is our modern day **magic wand**? It is the Light. The acronym for Light is *"Living in God's holy thoughts."* Why is this our magic wand? Because it is indestructible. It is always present. It defies the laws of the physical world as magical tools do. It is one of the major powers of the divine and, remember, we are Fairy Godmothers after all. It is faster than the speed of light and before you can see it coming or going, it is there. It can be summoned just by saying "Light" father (reference to God). That's pretty magical wouldn't you say? The more divine things are, the less you can actually see them. The Light is an extension of the "holy spirit" and like love, peace, joy and all the other attributes, we can't see the actual quality, just the results of it. The task of the Fairy Godmother is to focus on the unseen, for that is infinite, and not what can be seen, which ultimately will pass away. It is not necessary to see the Light, just trust that it is real and know it works. If you want to see it more often, it requires a certain trust in the divine and trust in the divine is absolutely part of the Fairy Godmother powers.

What is its effect in trying times? Trying times are marked by what is often called "the shadow." Another name for the negativity of the world is called the devil or evil. I am of the same thought as Harry Potter, which is we are better off just viewing it as ". . . he who shall not be named," Whatever we call it, when faced by the Light, evil and negativity leaves and dissolves into the Light. Where there is Light, there can be no dark. Only when the Light goes away, does the dark, (the shadow and negativity) come back.

We as Fairy Godmothers must keep our Light on. We must be ever vigilant at calling in the Light for the highest good. This occurs when we exercise our power of peace (the ceasing of being against anyone), for we are all God's children and our job is not to decide who is worth our care or who is not. Our job is to keep the Light within us and around us, and send it out to where it's needed.

Today's Fairy Godmother can activate her magic wand into an even more powerful tool by her ability *to see through the eyes of love, the innocence of every person she meets.* Divine innocence opens our hearts and sees into the hearts of others, allowing more healing, nurturing, joyful expression and encouragement for our community, our world and ourselves.

Our **magic words** are not "bibbity bobbity boo" anymore. There are several sets of tools because there are no "one size fits all" magic words. Our magic words will be as varied as the people who need them. One of my favorites is the *Peace Prayer*, which I learned from John-Roger at a seminar, *"God bless you, I love you. Peace, be still."* One of the most amazing experiences of how powerful the magic words work happened like this:

One night, my husband and I were awakened out of a deep sleep by people screaming and arguing. It seemed to be coming from our neighbors' backyard, which was adjacent to our backyard. It must have been 3:00 A.M. and we knew we wouldn't get back to sleep until it stopped. There didn't seem to be any physical violence other than the violence of their words so we did the next best thing. My husband and I joined hands, called in the Light and prayed, "Dear Father-Mother God, we ask for your love, light and peace, to fill, surround and protect us now. We ask also for your love, light and peace to go to the people who are in distress." We visualized a light, like a bubble, filling us and then moving to the other couple. We continued with the *Peace Prayer*, "God bless you, I love you. Peace, be still." Together, we recited it over and over again. After about five minutes, their voices subsided and, in a very short time, everything was still and quiet. We actually never heard them argue again.

I've repeated this several times with my family members as we are an emotional bunch. I just call in the Light for myself, see it flowing all around, through myself and into them, and quietly repeating the prayer with slower deeper breathing. It isn't long before emotions calm down. Kids are the easiest because they don't hang on to any of it. They get upset, the Light comes in, prayer goes out and without realizing it, and they are on to some new direction, a game or something else.

A friend once shared her story of the *Peace Prayer*. She and her husband always drove into the city to work. She found that she was often impatient with him and realized that she was judging him. It didn't feel right to her so she began to say the Peace Prayer to herself while they were traveling. About three weeks later, she noticed she wasn't anxious or judging him anymore. She had a perfectly calm and loving feeling toward her husband and they were getting along so much better. She confided that at first, she didn't actually feel much love, however over time the words still worked for her.

Another set of magic words were shared with me by Thomas One Wolf, a yogi and Tewa spiritualist from Taos, New Mexico, who I met while traveling with friends. He later came to California to visit me. I had an enchanting Fairy Godmother worthy little cabin in the woods at that time. We walked and talked and I shared my concerns about my family.

While strolling through the trees to the creek that ran near my cabin, Thomas shared a set of "magic words," which would change my life. I worried about everything; the environment, my family, my finances, my parents, and more. I thought that worrying was one of the ways I showed my love. Sound familiar? Thomas reminded me that to focus on the negative was like a negative prayer. When we are focused on the "worst-case scenario," we think that what we are doing is a form of caring. In reality, *what we focus on is what we create more of.* Thomas's magic words were *"Everything is as it should be."* Whenever I found myself taking on the weight of the world, these magic words would allow the space for a perfect effect to take place. They are both an affirmation and a reminder all at the same time.

Whenever I found myself caught by worry and fear, the thought of Thomas and his magic words, *"Everything is as it should be"* would come to mind. What was so special about those words? I would keep repeating the words to myself and actually began to calm down and think them through. Finally, I found the magic in the words. As we say them to ourselves, even in the midst of a challenging situation, the words become like a calming voice, a magic incantation to help us calm down, let go, and let God take care of things. In this way, we are turning it over to a higher power and not inserting our own ideas of what we think "should" be happening. Instead we are in acceptance. We can visualize a better scenario and create a matching feeling to bring forward a higher good. We as Fairy Godmothers always ask for the "highest good of all concerned" because we don't always know the details, but God does. It is our job to call for and send the light, in this way, we can enter into the Fairy Godmother quality of unconditional loving and acceptance. I am also constantly affirming to the universe, who is always listening, that *everything is as it should be,* and I trust that it then will be. It has been transformational for me, many times, and it can be for you too. For this is what we are called to do in service as Fairy Godmothers.

Another set of magic words that are a little longer than other magic words, however they work for me in times of extreme fear and panic and it is the *Lord's Prayer,* the 23rd Psalm, from the King James Version:

> *The lord is my shepherd, I shall not want.*
> *He maketh me to lie down in green pastures;*
> *He leadeth me beside the still waters.*
> *He restorath my soul.*
> *He leadeth me in the paths of righteousness for his name's sake.*
> *Yea, though I walk through the valley of the shadow of death,*
> *I will fear no evil; for thou are with me;*
> *Thy rod and thy staff they comfort me.*
> *Thou preparest a table before me in the presence of mine enemies;*
> *Thou anointest my head with oil; my cup runneth over.*
> *Surely goodness and mercy shall follow me all the days of my life;*
> *And I will dwell in the house of the lord forever and ever. Amen*

Lastly, but just as important is the magical tool of **fairy dust**. Fairy dust is the act of kindness. Kindness can disarm the most frightening person or situation imaginable. Kindness is so powerful it heals the giver, the receiver, and the one who witnesses its expression, as we discovered in our earlier chapter. Here is a story of kindness that had an unexpected ending.

Pickup in the Rain

One night, at 11:30 p.m., an elderly black woman was standing on the side of an Alabama highway trying to cope with a lashing rain storm. Her car had broken down and she desperately needed a ride. Soaking wet, she was trying to flag down a passerby. A young white man stopped to help her, which was generally unheard of in the racially conflicted 1960's. The man drove her to safety, helped her get assistance, and put her into a taxicab.

She seemed to be in a big hurry, but wrote down his address and thanked him. Seven days later, the man heard a knock on his door. To his surprise, a giant console color TV was delivered to his home. A special note was attached. It read:

"Thank you so much for assisting me on the highway the other night. The rain drenched not only my clothes, but also my spirits and then you came along. Because of you, I was able to make it to my dying husband's bedside just before he passed away. God bless you for helping me and unselfishly serving others."

Sincerely,
Mrs. Nat King Cole

The work we will be doing as Fairy Godmothers and Beary Godfathers today is soulful and sacred work, with a little whimsy, and a bit of magic and fairy dust mixed in, lest we take ourselves too seriously.

Our affirmation for this chapter:
I am infused with the magic of loving.

Questions to deepen your awareness:
1. What was your favorite fairy tale as a child and why?
2. Who are some of your heroes today and why?
3. If you could create a magical tool to use as a Fairy Godmother, what would it be and do?
4. Write about an experience of kindness that you've had.

Chapter 10

Tending the Garden
of Our Becoming

"The audacious hope of a single seed.
The audacious hope of rooted things."

~ CYNTHIA BOND, "RUBY"

We don't seem to have a lot of information on how fairy godmothers lived their lives when they weren't out answering the calls to serve, whether or not they went to school to learn magical incantations or how to find their perfect magic wand like Harry Potter.

As Fairy Godmothers, we must give from our overflow of love. If we are empty, what can we give? I have put together a way of preparing for our Fairy Godmother or Beary Godfather work in our world today. It is a way of loving ourselves in body, mind and emotions. Just like tending a magical garden, we must tend to our own inner and outer lives, with all the commitment, devotion and persistence of a gardener tending a very important garden, the garden of loving ourselves.

Just as the roots of trees hold moisture in the soil, grass and bushes keep the earth from washing away in a storm, doing these practices will help your most Beloved Self take root. It's never too late to love and care for ourselves.

Here are some ways to tend your garden:

Morning Practices

Morning Pages ~ Clearing
Affirmations ~ Intention
Mindset ~ Mental Clutter
Caring for our Body

Evening Practices

Evening Review ~ Journaling
Gratitude ~ Sleeping in Peace

Morning Practice: As you can see, there is more to do in the morning. In tending our garden, we come to it to take stock of anything that might have happened during the night. We take advantage of morning energies, pulling weeds and watering before the sun gets too high, and tend to garden predators like bugs and to the fence if necessary. We look at our garden as a whole and are able to see future projects as well.

All these ways, the morning and evening practices, make up the daily preparation of the Fairy Godmother. It sets the tone and direction of our day. With a conscious direction, we cannot help but accomplish our goals and dreams, discover and nourish our greatest potential. Whether you use it to become a consummate Fairy Godmother, or find a dream of something else, these morning practices will serve you with a more meaningful life. We will be looking more closely at our Spiritual practice in the next chapter.

Evening Practice: In the evening, we take stock of what will need weeding out (in the morning) and how our garden is growing. Although we have less to do, the evening practice is no less important.

Morning Practices

Morning Pages: They are just that. In Julia Cameron's book, *The Artist's Way*, she advocates that every morning, as part of our morning ritual, we write three 8 ½ x 11 inch pages of whatever comes into our minds. In this way we are clearing out mental clutter from the previous day. I find that as I do this, unfinished business from the day and night before comes out in my writing. I am able to look at it and put it on my to-do list or just completely let it go, because after all, I had a whole night to sleep on it and to see it with fresh eyes in the morning. If there is residual emotional stuff, I know I still have work to do on it, but I'm not hiding anything from myself. In this way we are more empty and available to spirit's call and direction. Morning pages is one of three writing processes. All are profoundly healing and supportive. We'll be covering the other writing exercises in-depth a little further on.

Affirmations: These are like the rows in our garden that separate the plant from the irrigation channels which nourish them. Without them, the seedlings could get washed away or receive no life giving water. Affirmations help us live out our intentions, and keep us focused on our main goals and outcomes. Perhaps we have a quality we are trying to embody more. An affirmation helps us to focus more clearly and specifically on what we want to create. Without them we might drift with no direction, and there's nothing like having a good reason to get up in the morning (other than go to work).

Affirmations give order to our garden, to the new lives and sense of purpose we are shaping. We affirm our ability to find ways to express them more. When we don't have a course to steer by, a channel for our energy and love to flow through, we fall prey to our old ideas and patterns, our default thinking and actions, you know, the ones we had before we decided to become Fairy Godmothers and Beary Godfathers. The patterns of depression, loneliness, fearful thinking, taking things personally and patterns from our childhood can creep in.

Using affirmations helps us to guard against the unproductive, habitual patterns of negative thinking that for so long have ruled us. We now realize we don't want to think these thoughts or continue to express in these ways, but we're just so used to them, they have become our "norm" for responses. Now we are creating a new "norm" of non-reactivity, peace and calm.

Clear affirmations help us to not allow the old, unproductive thoughts to keep us small and unfulfilled. The great philosopher, Ralph Waldo Emerson, said, *"Stand guard at the portal of your mind."*

At the end of each chapter, as you've noted, I have created an affirmation that inspires me and I encourage you to make use of them yourself or create one of your own. State what you want to create or change, and begin the statement with "I am . . ."

The creative power within us is harnessed through using the words "I am . . ." followed by whatever our affirmation is, as a creative statement. That creative statement has power, and lays the ground work for manifesting our intention. Affirmations are the tools of our intentions and clarity is everything. Below is a creative strategy, a recipe for creating anything you want:

1. Clarity of intention,
2. Consistent affirmation,
3. Taking action,
4. Visualizing the end result,
5. Gratitude for success even before it has happened.

In this case, we as Fairy Godmothers are the inspiration, and have the ability and joy of bringing more love and peace into our world.

Intentions: Creating through our intentions is like harnessing the creative force of the universe. God is Intention. God makes our garden grow. What we want to harvest will come out of the clarity of our intention. It is the soul of all consistent endeavor, the power of the universe dressed in words.

"Intentions compressed into words enfold magic powers."

~ DEEPAK CHOPRA

First we decide what our intention is. Then as we use our affirmations to train our minds and emotions to be tuned to its creation, our intentions become a manifest reality.

Remember what the book of Genesis 1:3 says, "God said let there be light and there was light". This was God's intention manifest, and it came dressed in the words of his affirmation and empowered by his Almighty power, and that is the power of intention. We also can use the same practice.

Mindset: On the surface, positive thinking helps our frame of mind, our attitude, what we say, do, and how we do it. It's much more than feeling good about ourselves, energetic, etc. Mindset helps us create and build skills that will help us throughout our lifetime while consistently adding value to it.

How is it that some people do much better in spite of their talents and abilities? Research tells us that it's the way we think about our abilities that makes the difference. Having the belief that you are in control of your own ability and can be as successful as you want, that's a mindset. We can have a fixed mindset that falls apart when it doesn't come out the way we think it "should". Or we can have a growth mindset which is open to new and different ways to deal with life. This well-worn and often told story is about a creature that by all odds would never "beat" his opponent but he believed he could and so he never gave up.

The Tortoise and the Hare

One day, the slow moving, ordinary tortoise came upon the hare, a fast and confident braggart of a being and asked him to have a race with him. The hare was so confident that he would beat the tortoise in a race that after the race started, he found a comfortable little niche and he laid back and went to sleep.

The tortoise, on the other hand, continued toward the finish line, tramping along at tortoise speed, but he never lost sight of where he wanted to go.

The tortoise believed that he had a chance of winning if he just kept going. When the hare awoke, he started running as fast as he could but he never caught up to the tortoise and so the tortoise won the race.

The hare had a **fixed mindset**. He believed that his ability would always mean that he would win at whatever he did, so he didn't have to keep focused.

The tortoise had a **growth mindset**. He believed that if he worked hard and kept going, he would win. He was also not afraid to take a risk, or he would never have thought he had a chance to win a race with the hare.

People with a fixed mindset can easily get discouraged by setbacks, be frustrated and run the risk of just giving up and then finally they do just give up. Those with a growth mindset view a setback as a challenge and opportunity to learn. They tend to try harder in an effort to overcome the obstacle and achieve their goal.

Let's also have a mindset that allows for mistakes, because making mistakes is how we find the right way to go. They are only course corrections. A positive mindset sees that if we just do the best we can and decide to learn from it all, we will be triumphant.

For Fairy Godmothers, that means if we don't succeed as much as we would like one day, we go optimistically into the next with a greater awareness of what worked and what distracted us. Notice, I never mentioned failure. The only failure is to give up. We go forward, stepping out into what could be viewed as the unknown, until we do it a few times. Then it is no longer unknown. With the correct attitude and mindset, it becomes our universe of unlimited possibilities, and that is definitely Fairy Godmother territory. Our possibility is to create a more peaceful and loving world to live in for us and everyone else.

The power to think positively is greatly enhanced when you are able to catch yourself when you aren't. According to a recent study, our genes influence about 50% of the variation in our personal happiness and circumstances, while only 10% comes from our income and environment. That means 40% is based on our daily activities and the conscious choices we make. The good news is that our actions really can make all the difference in the world, our world.

Affirmations and intentions help us keep the flow of the positive going in our garden. Being aware when we are not positive is like us weeding our garden, so that our harvest will be magnificent.

Clearing Clutter: Another "weeding" activity is clearing our mental clutter. It is a fact that no two thoughts can maintain the same space in your mind at the same time, which is why life becomes a matter of choices. Clutter is anything that stands in the way of what matters to you, what's important. Our brains are constantly on overload. We might try to focus on affirmations or positive imagery, but some negative thought, or some unpleasant memory creeps in and we find ourselves struggling with it and we can't just wish it away. It takes concentrated effort to clean house, clear out the clutter of our mind. Here are some strategies:

Address the Mess: When we leave tasks unfinished tasks such as the dishes you haven't done yet, stop, and do them. If there are things around the house or yard that need work, do one task a day or get some help especially if it's a big job. It will seem less tedious if you break it down into manageable pieces.

We all know what children are like. They have boundless energy, they tend to live in the now, for the moment, and view life like a big game to play and most don't seem to have a care in the world.

One thing that sets their boundless energy apart from our more weighty life is that we often hang on, but also, we have all these threads of unfinished tasks. The unconscious makes a note in energy terms, of all the things you have started and not finished. Everything from books half read, to cleaning out the closet of clothes you know you will never wear again, projects you started but never finished.

Yes our priorities change, but the unconscious does not forget. All these uncompleted things are pieces of your energy being held in the unconscious waiting to be resumed and used. Energy you could use to enhance your daily life right now. Some people have reported that after cleaning out their garage they actually lost a few pounds and slept better, wow. Now that's a blessing in disguise.

Maybe you decide you don't want to do a certain project anymore or you didn't like that book you started and you don't care about finishing it, that's energy being held in "limbo." Declare it completed and move on and you will get your energy back.

Give the "half done" projects to someone else to do, a Girl or Boy Scout Troop, a neighbor who tinkers or sews, or the old tried and true, sell it at a garage sale. Now we have on-line garage sales, known as e-bay and craigslist, (www.ebay.com and www.craigslist.org).

I guarantee you will see a marked change in your energy. More energy to take care of yourself, your home, etc. More energy to express your joy and more energy to inspire your good works as a Fairy Godmother.

Emotional Clutter: Unaddressed emotional feelings can also distract us and they can even back up on us. They take their toll on our attitude and can also lead to depression if not attended to. Journaling and "free form writing" are some of the most effective ways to deal with unresolved emotional feelings and issues. These two practices can clear these distracting and exhausting energies, so can forgiveness which we will visit later.

Negative Self-Talk: This too is a part of emotional clutter. Whether it's self judgment because you forgot to do something or you are beating up on yourself for past mistakes, here's something that works for me.

Have the intention to catch yourself when you are talking down, criticizing, "shoulding" or "guilting" yourself. This can be done as a morning or evening practice or just when it comes up. Take a moment, sit down with a sheet of paper, either fold it or mark it into two halves. Write down the negative self-talk on the left side of the page, then on the right, opposite side of the paper, create a corresponding positive statement and write it down on the right side, to counteract it.

It might look something like this:

Negative Self-Talk	Positive Self-Talk
I am late.	I am developing perfect timing now.
I hate my life today.	Everything is as it should be.
Why is there so much violence in the world?	Today, I am peaceful and calm.

As you go over your statements there will be a noticeable pattern. As you create affirmations for them, you might notice there is a recurring emotional theme, associated with your negative self-talk and/or sometimes even a memory from childhood or a stressful time from the past. As you create your opposite positive self-talk, the old thinking, patterns, and feelings will start to fall away. It also makes you more conscious of your self-talk.

I have affirmations for most all of my shadow (negative) self-talk. Because I came from a very poor and dysfunctional beginning, I would always feel like I was not enough or I would never be enough or have enough. This was a childhood decision and for most of my younger adult life, it was true, a self-fulfilling prophesy, so I created an affirmation to replace the shadow self-talk, *"I am beautiful, capable, lovable, and one with all my good and prosperity."* I still use this one all the time.

One of the reasons I use "one with my good. . . ." is because if we always see our dreams "out there," we will always be chasing them, out there. In order to receive them, make them your own, you must bring them home, own them, and one of the ways I have found that worked is to claim what I want as me "being one with my. . . ."

I shared my story a few chapters back. As a child I believed I was ugly and defective and that nobody liked me and I didn't fit in . . . This affirmation counteracts those thoughts too. I have used this affirmation for years, and although I have done a lot of reframing and soul searching, I still sometimes find myself going into those thoughts of lack and self judgment. Then I stop, pull my affirmation forward in my consciousness, and tell myself, in the mirror if possible, at least 10 times. It always works and you can create one that works for you.

One of the most common ways and times I use this particular affirmation is when I start feeling anxious about a gathering I'm speaking at or a meeting. The negative self-talk starts up, chipping away at my self-esteem, self-doubt starts coming up, and this issue of not being enough surfaces. Again, I start telling myself my affirmation as I am driving, on the way to the meeting. By the time I get there, I have changed my state back into confidence and loving. My expression and my feelings match my positive affirmation. I am back on track with my confidence and my conviction that I am doing my purpose. It really works.

Roadblocks for Prevention: We can create mental roadblocks to prevent the mental clutter and negative self-talk from taking hold. Using affirmations and seeing ourselves doing the thing we are working on as completed and well done, is one such roadblock. It prevents us from falling into the old negative thoughts. We can start putting up little notes to ourselves, with our affirmations and intentions. I like to write little love notes to myself and leave them where I will find them.

You can put post-its of your affirmations on the bathroom mirror. I like to keep them on 3 x 5 cards in my car to take out and look at while I'm waiting at a stop light or to look at while sitting in my car getting ready to leave.

I keep them by my bed to look at before I drop off to sleep. This is particularly effective because the half hour before we fall asleep, our unconscious mind is listening. That is why you don't want to fall asleep watching the news or a violent show on TV. I have them posted in my office and on my refrigerator door.

Making a collage, or vision card with pictures is a very powerful way to address monitoring and re-directing ourselves and tons of fun too. You can make one for you as the Fairy Godmother, happily doing some act of kindness or sharing. Find pictures of world peace, happy families, and communities coming together.

Compartmentalize: This can be achieved by noticing negative thoughts and just setting them aside, letting them go. Perhaps it's a thought about things you have to do by Friday. Make a list of those things and put them on a to-do list. This gets them off your mind so you can be in the present. Then later, look at these items as unfinished business and decide when you will complete them, and then follow through. This is how we build trust in ourselves and also build confidence. If you want to free up energy, complete everything you start or decide that you aren't going to and declare it done and let it go.

Much research has been done that informs us that if you don't write it down, it won't get done so we make our "to-do" list, a plan for the day, week and even the month. Once we put it on the list, we can notice any negativity towards a task or quality in ourselves. Then we can make an affirmation to address the issue, set our intention, act on it, then let go and let God.

Caring for Your Body: We've all heard the idea that our body is a temple. I didn't start out with that idea. As a child I had so many disabilities I believed my body wasn't very good, nor did it work very well. No one talked to me about my feelings so I just stuffed them. As time went by I learned to speak well by singing in choir at school. I strengthened my legs and hips by riding my bicycle.

One day when I was eight years old, even upon threat of a beating, I threw my crutches down and told my mom I was never going to use them again. She just threw up her hands, picked up the crutches and I never saw them again and. . . . I never needed them again. You might say I just "grew out of them", grew out of my disabilities. Life was calling me, and even at eight years of age, I knew I wanted to go. I wasn't going to allow life to pass me by as a crippled victim, which is probably just what my mother thought I was, or at least that's what my life looked like back then.

We are holistic beings. We have physical, mental, emotional, and spiritual aspects that make up our "earth suit", the vehicle for our souls. Because of this, we must love our bodies too. We must take care of them, nourish, rest, and exercise them. We Fairy Godmothers must cherish our bodies as we cherish our souls. When we do this, we are also creating the awareness of how important it is to care for our bodies to those around us and then everyone is healthier and everyone wins.

We can't do our fairy godmother service if we are not healthy enough to do the physical activity. To give service, we must also be emotionally balanced, and mentally clear, so that our spirits can shine through. I know that some of us do have trouble getting out like we used to, and there are still ways to be our Fairy Godmother selves despite our physical state, but we still have to love and care for our bodies. Especially if they are in need of attention.

If God didn't want us to love our bodies as well as our spirits, there would be no joy of movement like dancing. There would be no ecstatic experience through sexuality. There would be no "runners high", endorphins released, serotonin-induced healing in our immune system. God is in everything and every-one, so we learn to love it all.

First and foremost we must love our body "no matter what"—fat, thin, old, crippled, sick, well, short, tall, wild hair or no hair. It is the only body we have this life, so let's treat it like it's the sacred temple it is. In taking care of our bodies there are certain priorities, here are some of the most basic and important to me.

Water: Science says that we are about 70% water. It takes water to lubricate our joints, run our elimination systems, it even takes water to run our nervous system. By the end of the day, even your sleep is affected by hydration.

Hospitals often see many older patients for dehydration. Experts say to drink an 8 oz. glass of water the first thing upon arising in the morning, it helps clear out our elimination system. Then about 30 minutes before a meal, it aids digestion, and last but not least, if we have another glass of water 30 minutes before bedtime, it can help us sleep better.

Another positive water rule for hydration is to drink one ounce per every two pounds of body weight. So if you weigh 150 pounds, you optimally should drink 75 ounces. For me, if I just drink two whole 28 ounce bottles, I feel pretty good. As you go along you will discover your perfect balance.

Nutrition is also important but so specific in its very nature, varying from person to person, including medical advice notwithstanding. But with all that said, here are some things that have worked for me.

Less sugar is better, any sugar substitute that contains aspartame or a derivative is very toxic. I use Stevia, it's natural and comes in organic form. Minerals, including trace minerals are imperative, some can be provided by using Himalayan pink salt. Lemons are a miracle food, they alkalize the body's PH, provide Vitamin C, every organ in the body likes it.

Be sure to get enough protein, and especially if you are more physically active. It can be gotten through rice and beans, some green vegetables and of course our usual animal protein. Smoothies made with plant protein are great and can be made to be more of a desert, what's not to love about that.

Last but not least. It's still true, an apple a day can keep the doctor away as a general rule and a green salad every day (unless allergic), etc., does too. Green tea is good for the heart. You can research this information online or check with your doctor as to what is best for you.

I'm not a doctor nor a nutritionist but I have learned a few things along the way, in life and I'm just passing it on. I hope you use any of this information for your highest and best health. I do want all my Fairy Godmothers to be healthy, we are whole beings after all.

Breathe: There are so many disciplines for breathing now, they're on the internet, in books, part of yoga, etc. Breathing is a major component of "Heart Math", a system of stress reduction. I have found that just by slowing my breathing down and breathing deeper into my belly, I can calm down.

One of the breathing exercises that I do as I get ready to meditate, I learned from John-Roger, on his Meditation CD called "Meditation for Peace".

It goes something like this: I sit up straight in a chair. Close my eyes and take a deep breath in, for a count of five, then I hold this breath for the count of five and then let it out for the count of five then release any residual breath for a count of five. I do this five times. A variation I added, from what I learned from the Heart Math Institute, is to focus on my heart as I breathe, as though I am breathing into and through my heart. I find I am calm and centered within myself by the end of this exercise and I'm ready to meditate. If you do yoga, each yoga move has a breathing sequence. When we get upset, frightened, we tend to freeze up, breath shallowly and then we can't think straight, we start being reactive, and it's all downhill from there. Breathing is God's gift to us, it is our life line, not only physically, but I have found it to be a life line to the divine.

Exercise: The more we move our bodies, the better they work. Movement helps us to strengthen our muscles, lubricate our joints, and just plain loosen up our bodies. Stretching exercises also help our nervous systems too, not to mention staving off depression.

One of my favorite ways to move is to swim and do water aerobics. I am weightless in the water, and when they play music, it is an effortless dance routine. Walking in nature is very healing for me, with or without your I-pod. I don't take my iPod because I want to hear the sweet voices of the birds, and be available to chat along the walking path with people I meet. It's a great way to Fairy Godmother, spread joy, give attention and appreciation while nourishing our natural beingness.

There are a lot of gyms out there, most community centers have exercise programs and pools. Senior Centers, the Boys and Girls clubs and the YMCA have all kinds of reasonable, if not free, programs.

If you are at a place where your mobility is limited, these centers have classes for chair yoga, gentle stretching, stationary bikes, etc. I have been physically limited at times in my life, and I found that even if I just moved a little bit, a little at a time, I always felt better. The more I did, the better I felt and the less pain I had. We must move our bodies every day, or we could lose the ability to move them, and I don't want that for any of us Fairy Godmothers and Beary Godfathers.

Evening Practices

Evening Review: It's a practice that for me has helped keep many a fitful night from ever happening. As you lay in bed, quietly waiting for sleep but before you drop off, this exercise will erase the blackboard of your mind and emotions and leave you more peaceful and better able to navigate the next day, when similar things come up.

In your mind, go back over your day. I like to start from the A.M. Each memory of the day you have . . . running an errand, walking the dog, a phone call that didn't go well, difference of opinion with a family member, etc. Replay in your mind the experience, only in your mind, imagine it happening in a calm, cooperative, peaceful way, you at your best, and them at their best, all through the day. If you forgot something, imagine you didn't forget it, see yourself following through. Along the way, anytime you find yourself judging yourself or the other person or situation, just forgive yourself now. Forgive the judgment on yourself and on them. By the time you get to the end of your day in your mind, you will have cleared the negativity and fear and arrived in your imagination, at the end, guilt free, lovingly embracing it all.

Journaling: Get at least two journals. One for your everyday entries and one for your Fairy Godmother entries. Write in your journal every day, even if it's only a sentence or two. Write about your feelings, your thoughts, a new experience you had. You can ask yourself questions in your journal, give yourself a day to process the question, then write what comes up for you. You can write down any regrets and any thoughts about them, disappointments, etc.

Last but not least, keep a Fairy Godmother Journal where you write down your everyday offerings and your "ah-ha" moments. Celebrate what you did to spread love, caring and sharing and kindness. Keep track of all you do, if you miss a day of going out, you'll get to it the next day. Your Fairy Godmother journal is your celebration and your support and encouragement.

I also like to write down my dreams, you could get a journal for dreams also. You can track dreams by journaling them, and you will find connections and patterns and even premonitions sometimes. The best time for dream journaling is just when you wake, while they are fresh in your mind, and before you move into your day and the world wipes them away. As you do this, you will start remembering them more. The gold of your soul is often stored in your unconscious as dreams. Your dream memories may be sparse in the beginning but the more consistently you journal them, the more you will remember and it is also a very healing journey. You will find that as you get in the habit of doing this, you will be revealing yourself more deeply to yourself.

Journaling is the gift we give ourselves, it can bring healing, revelation, and new understandings about yourself and your life. It is a way of embracing yourself with understanding and listening to parts of yourself that maybe you had never heard before.

When you get a chance to get together with others in your community who are joining in with Fairy Godmothering, you can share from your journal. These are wonderful ways to include your joy in your Fairy Godmother work/play.

Gratitude and Sleeping in Peace: Every one of us has down days, stressful days that we inevitably take with us to bed. We've talked about our evening review and it is a great tool for letting it all go and bringing us back into a better internal sense of balance and peace.

One of the unmistakable signs that there is a lack of peace is the lack of peaceful sleep. That is why I put these two side by side. The gift of gratitude and its effect on our peace is amazing. I have found it to be one of the best "sleep aids" I've ever found.

Here is my practice for both, sleep and gratitude. After I've done my evening review, and sleep is out there somewhere, just out of reach and I'm trying to lure it in, I turn to "gratitude". I pull back inside myself, focus on my heart area, tap my heart with my finger, and begin to breathe into my heart center. As I get the breath going, slowly, in and out of my heart, I start thinking of all the things I have to be grateful for. I add in things I appreciate about people and situations in my life. It isn't long before I notice it's getting light out and my night of sleep in the arms of God has come and gone.

It is a blessing you can give to yourself. Also, if you find yourself waking up in the middle of the night, that's a great time to pray for those people and places in your life and the world that are in need.

There are times though, when I am still awake and I just go back over what I am grateful for and what I appreciate in my life.

Don't leave yourself out of this prayer of gratitude, be grateful for your commitment to caring for yourself, and the love you have for the pets, your partner, your family and people you have in your life.

Gratitude is like the essence of God, when it is present, our hearts are open, receiving God's grace. Be grateful for the grace.

After we do all these evening practices, we will sleep in the arms of love, and rest in the peace of God. And I wish that for all beings, and for my Fairy Godmothers.

We are whole and holy beings. Fairy Godmothers must remember that life is moving, vibrant, and all around us, so let's celebrate it with our bodies, minds and hearts. It will help us to share more love.

In closing I'd like to add that with all these suggestions for living a healthy, self-caring life, the sheer number of action steps can be overwhelming. So let me just say, some practices are every day, some may apply only in times of stress (like free form writing). All are intended to make you more mindful that the more and better you love and take care of yourself, the more ease, grace and well-being you will have in your life . . . and the more able you will be to share your love, peace and kindness in our world.

Loving the world begins with loving ourselves. You cannot give what you don't have. In our next chapter we are going to connect with the ways we can immerse ourselves, consciously, in the energy of Love, which to me, is being enfolded by the Soul nourishing experience of divine love, the love of God.

Our affirmation for this chapter:
I am happy, healthy, and inspired, living my life with joy and enthusiasm in my whole being.

Questions to deepen your awareness:
1. What do I want to release from my emotions so that I can celebrate my life more fully?
2. What does it feel like to sleep in the arms of the Lord?
3. What's one thing I can do to take better care of my body?

Chapter 11

Nourishing Our Spiritual Potential ~ a Soulful Task

"Love is the experience we all have when we open our hearts enough that the energy of God, spirit, can flow through it."

~ MICHAEL SINGER

As Fairy Godmothers, we need to fill our internal reservoirs with love. This can only be done by ourselves. Yes, others will respond to the love we are sending and using and this sustains us to a degree, but they cannot fill us completely from the outside in. It is an inside endeavor. The good news is no matter how busy we get in the world, we can and must step back into our own inner sanctuary and fill our own cup. I have found some techniques that have worked very well for me and I hope, in sharing them with you, you will have the success I have.

Finding the right balance between our physical and spiritual self is one of the most challenging aspects of our existence, but it is a worthy task. To maximize our potential is to understand and know why we are here in the first place. That question can also be, *what is the meaning of life?* Some people believe that we are here to be all that we can be. I encourage you to write in your journal, the answers that come up for you to these questions. What do you believe about God, what do you believe about love, and why you are here? These questions can lead to a deeper connection to the divine within us. It is from this place we will find the strength, love and light to carry us into our calling as Fairy Godmothers.

I believe we are here to learn to love ourselves unconditionally and to love others without exception. At this time in my existence, I personally believe that I came to embrace myself as the Beloved and make every effort to share that love with humanity. I am still discovering what it looks like in my very core and what it looks like manifested in my daily life as a Fairy Godmother.

The last chapter was about our everyday activities for taking care of ourselves physically, mentally, and emotionally so we are self-supporting in our Fairy Godmothering. This also applies to nurturing our spiritual lives because we are holistic beings.

This chapter is about the more subtle, although powerful, realities like love, cherishing, inner peace, joy, enthusiasm, and inspiration.

We don't really see God face to face, but I believe we can know God heart to heart. We can feel God and love through our emotions as inspiration. We are going to look at cultivating an inner knowing of God, heart to heart, every day, at work, at play, at rest and connecting to our deep inner knowing of God, as the Beloved. I find for myself that the more I embrace myself as the Beloved, the more love I have to share with others in our world and I believe this is how we can transform it.

There has been much written about the meaning of the word Beloved as it applies to the spiritual life in ancient texts. My understanding of the Beloved is that it is another way to know and understand God within us. We are all Beloved. We are all seeking the Beloved and for the most part, until recently, we've misunderstood its infinite presence. For many of us it has been about finding our perfect mate or partner or that unique something outside of ourselves.

The Beloved can be embodied by our true love and the greater reality is that it is a mirror of our own Beloved within, the very core of our Being, the God within us. At least this is what I have learned and I am always seeking to experience more of it. I encourage you to seek the Beloved inside of you and then you will know the Beloved in the way that is perfect for you.

Whatever your search for God and life's meaning is, whether you are inspired by the mystery of science or some awesome view of the horizon, these mysteries can be humbling, mystifying, and when we see them, experience them, they are the foundations of a spiritual life that can open us up to experiencing more of the path that one follows in search of God within.

Here are the main ways that I have found works for me when nourishing myself spiritually:

- Making a connection through meditation.
- Joy, inspiration and humor.
- Forgiveness as a spiritual practice.
- Free form writing as a spiritual practice.
- The Fairy Godmother Code as a prayer of affirmation.

Heart Breath Meditation and Connecting with the Wisdom of the Heart: This meditation is a practice of the divine truth that love will go where we direct it and we'll be making good use of this awareness. Find a quiet and comfortable place to sit, preferably with your feet on the floor and your back as straight as possible.

Start all meditations by calling in the Light. This is my prayer:

"Dear Father-Mother God,

Beloved of my Soul, I ask just now to be filled, surrounded and protected by your Love, Light and Peace . . . I visualize a pure white light coming down from above my head, flowing throughout my body, then spiraling around it and at the end, I see a gold umbrella pop out over me which is how I see the divine protection of God."

Now you can begin your journey by setting the intention to connect from within to God or whatever outcome you choose for this meditation.

- Start by taking a deep breath in for a count of five and then holding it for a count of five and then let it go, slowly, for another count of five, completely emptying for another count of five. Do this five times.
- In this way, you let go of the world and focus only on breathing. Let that be all there is. Just breathe and become consciously aware of your breath.
- Next, place your hand on your heart center and take three deep breaths. With each breath in, with intention, pull the feeling and energy of love into your heart.
- As you breathe back out of your heart, state your intention of *peace* by connecting to the word or experience of peace as you breathe out of your heart. This can be done three times or until you feel connected to your love more consciously.
- Next, turn your attention to something you are grateful for while you continue breathing. Expand your feelings of gratitude to include someone you love, someone dear to your heart. It could be your partner, your child, a pet, your grandchild, a garden you love, your spiritual leader or teacher. Whatever opens your heart.
- After a few minutes, take this loving energy and send it up to your head, where your mind is. Let the love bathe your thoughts and then allow your breath to flow out through the top of your head as you exhale. Then begin the process all over again. Do this for a few minutes. You will find your heart and your mind filled with loving energy. This is you attuning to your spiritual connection.

- Finally, there will come an inner pause or a deeper relaxation, this is your sign to just let go and breathe normally. This is the time you can just float on the divine silence of your soul. With our prayer, breathing with intentions, we have been seeking God. Now is the time to surrender to the divine energy within us. At this time, you may be receptive to divine guidance and inspiration or a deep sense of peace.

After floating for a while, you can send light and love out to people and places in your family, community, and even the world. It may take some practice to get to that deep connection with your Beloved, your center of love, but practice makes perfect.

How can you be a Fairy Godmother from across the world? By sending your love and quiet prayers to places in distress.

At this point, I send the Light out and see the places and people filled with it. You can also place columns of Light in places, homes, etc. for the greatest good of all. I might do this with a recitation like this:

"Dear Father-Mother God,

I ask for a column of light to be placed at (name a place) and let it extend deep into the heart of mother earth and up into the heart of God for the highest good of all, to bring blessings of health, happiness, peace and well-being."

This part is totally up to your own creation as well as how and what you send. I always end with the words ". . . *and so it is, Amen.*"

Joy and Inspiration: Joy and inspiration are matters of the heart. We are all inspiration seekers. We enjoy inspiring books about history, movies, stories, and songs. Through them, we connect with our more expanded feelings.

Experiencing joy and inspiration can bring healing to us. When we are feeling inspired, endorphins and serotonin flow through our system.

You can't be depressed at the same time you are inspired. Inspiration causes our hearts to open, our hopes to soar, our bodies to react favorably, which causes us to be infused by the healing chemicals that are already within us and waiting to be released. These reactions can bring healing such as lifting our moods, boosting our immune system, dispelling depression, and helping us to feel happy.

Another inspiring activity is viewing art that we love, whether it is paintings at a museum, ceramics, or glassware at State fair or festival. Going to inspirational movies or concerts, even viewing them at home can inspire us. I love Super Soul Sunday with Oprah Winfrey, on the OWN network. I record them so I can take an inspirational break every day. I will sit with my favorite cup of tea, lunch or a snack, relax and surrender to the inevitable joy, hope, and love of being inspired.

Humor: Laughter is very healthy. Have you ever noticed when spirit is really present, so is joyful laughter. I appreciate Charles M. Schultz's words:

> *"If I were given the opportunity to present a gift to the next generation, it would be the ability for each individual to laugh at himself."*

Norman Cousins, also famous for his work with humor and laughter, began his personal journey as a serious, stressed out business man. As a result, he contracted a very debilitating disease, which completely took over his life and would invariably kill him. After suffering with no relief in sight, the doctors believed that there was nothing more they could do for him. Faced with his own mortality, Cousins began soul searching. He looked at how his attitudes (critical, negative thinking, competitiveness) might be influencing his current misery.

Norman decided that if he was going to go out, he was going to go out laughing. He started watching non-stop TV and videos of the comedians of his day. Sometimes he laughed so much that his stomach muscles and ribs hurt, but within months, he regained some of his mobility and diffused some of his pain. It wasn't long before he was actually pain-free and ultimately was completely healed just from laughing and choosing to be happy. Watching humorous YouTube.com videos is a favorite de-stressor for my husband and I love to hear him laughing out loud.

I always enjoy reading the Reader's Digest section, "Laughter is the Best Medicine." I've learned that it really is. Humor works and so do pets. Why am I talking so much about de-stressing? Because stress can literally inhibit your immune system, cause pain, contribute to depression, and cause more colds and healing takes longer.

Joy of Pets: My husband's job is stressful at times. He comes home from these particularly trying days and he's not a happy camper. His nerves are on edge. He's wound up. On nights like this, he sits down on the floor with our dogs, starts rolling around with them, and within 15 minutes, he is calm, relaxed and has forgotten all about the job. We call our pets our *Thera-pups*.

Pets are joyful little creatures and dogs are great when you need some exercise, too. They can get you out of the house when no one else can. They demonstrate unconditional love and joy. Who doesn't want that? Unconditional love and the quality of joy are attributes of the Soul and they are qualities of a Fairy Godmother's heart.

Now you may wonder why, especially if you are not a happy pet owner, pet experiences would appear in the chapter on spirituality? Well, on behalf of my inner Fairy Godmother, dog spelled backwards is GOD. I rest my case with a bit of humor.

Forgiveness: I view forgiveness as a sacred practice. Sacred because it re-connects us to the divine within us. Forgiveness cleans our spirit and un-clutters our minds and emotions. It makes us more available to the love that we are so we can give of our love more freely. We all are learning and growing in our awareness of love and kindness. Sometimes, we are not able to live as lovingly as we might want to. In those times, we forgive ourselves for what-ever we did that missed the mark, and forgive any judgment we have against ourselves for it.

The hidden treasure in forgiving self, which has been referred to as "the keys to the kingdom," is to accept ourselves and what we did. Only after we accept ourselves, can we truly be forgiven. The bible alludes to forgiveness when it says, "Go forward and sin no more." I interpret it to mean, yes, we had an error in judgment, a moment of carelessness, but we are still divine, no matter what, because we are loved by our creator, no matter what.

When we forgive ourselves and the person who wronged us, and forgive the judgment of it, we are released. Judgment, revenge, and regret are like the glue of sorrow. If we hold on to these thoughts and emotions, we are stuck with it, but if we forgive, we are absolved of it. Having released it, we begin the process of healing through what is left, acceptance and love, for ourselves and others. We all know that horrendous loss can devastate our lives, but it is through forgiveness that we are restored, set free. When we forgive, it doesn't mean that we agree with the violence or we forget. It just means we are let-ting the negative go. Forgiveness is what we do to love ourselves back into wholeness.

Here is one of my favorite ways to perform the sacred practice of forgive-ness. I am quiet, sitting comfortably, and know that I am preparing to talk to God. I take some deep breaths so that I go to a place of inner peace and I begin with this prayer.

"Dear Father-Mother God, Beloved of my Soul,

I ask for the clearing (I pause to receive it-it's like waiting for your prayer request to be received in advance). I ask for your love, light, peace and grace to fill, surround, and protect me . . . (I see and visualize it happening in-side me). I ask also for it to fill, surround and protect . . . (say their name or the situation). I forgive myself for judging myself and judging them for (whatever the judgment is about) and I ask that all negativity be dissolved in your unconditional loving. I gratefully go freely into the rest of my life, and may they go freely also. God bless us all, for the highest good of all.

And so it is. Amen."

You can create your own personal forgiveness prayer, the most important thing is that you do the forgiveness and use the Light to release it.

When we judge someone, we are actually judging ourselves, too. We Fairy Godmothers are not set up to be judge and jury. We are here to bring more love and kindness into the world. One of the ways we do this is practicing forgiveness, even for the angry, violent things we see on the news. We ask that the Light be there, that grace prevails and love enfolds us and the world.

If I find myself still stewing and angry about something or someone, I know there is more to do. I need to release the angst and negativity so that I can go deeper into forgiveness. A very effective way to release negative emotions is explained in the next section called Free Form Writing.

Another technique I have discovered is to imagine the experience and/or person in a more balanced light, replacing the "bad" memory with a good one. I imagine myself doing it all differently, creating no errors or mistakes. I visualize whatever happened in the best light that I can and see the other person doing the same, working for the betterment of both of us. I have found that it really frees up positive energy and opens the way for forgiveness so you don't repeat the mistake going forward. It also creates a space for the more uplifted experience to happen.

Why would you think this is possible? We have separate bodies, individual thoughts and feelings, don't we? The science of Quantum Physics has now proven that we are connected. That a small group of people with one accord has the ability to affect a greater number of people around them.

If you think that you can harbor ill will toward someone and get away with it cleanly, think again. What we carry in our hearts, think in our thoughts and the feelings we experience are transmitted on the same level. So, if you keep love in your heart, good thoughts, and loving kindness in your emotions, you will be protected because there will be no opening for the negative to take root.

In the teachings of the Native Americans, it is referred to as the great web of life. In Matthew 25:40; Christ said it this way, *"Inasmuch as you have done it to the least one of these, and you have done it unto me."* He knew that we are all connected as human beings and we human beings are all connected to Him. So, send love and Light to your enemies. They may have a crisis of conscience or surrender to their better nature, we don't know the big picture or see the future, however God does. We only know our part and I find that knowing my part is all I need to know because that is all the power I have.

Love is the most powerful thing we can bring to any situation, i.e., our personal daily issues and those we see in our communities. We are all souls struggling to be loved. Where there is great violence, there is great fear. What fear needs most is love. Fear is a call for love and divine Light. We as Fairy Godmothers have our work cut out for us, don't we?

Free Form Writing: Is another sacred practice because it restores our center and reconnects us with God. I love the phrase, *heart to heart with God.* It is our nature that spirituality is our most natural way of being. It was in the beginning when we were born in innocence and it will be in the end when we go home, to the Light, to God in heaven where there is only love.

This exercise is one of the most effective tools I have found for releasing anger and other intense emotions. Although it is simple, do not be deceived. It is a deep and soulful act of cleansing and it is very effective. I learned this practice on my spiritual journey with John-Roger. You can find it in his book, *Spiritual Warrior* by John-Roger, DSS. This is how it works:

- Find a quiet place to write. Get a big yellow pad (my favorite) and a pen not a pencil-you don't want to interrupt the writing flow with a broken lead, etc. You want to "let it all out." Light a candle to absorb excess emotional energy and do a little prayer of gratitude for clarity. Do the exercise for at least 20 minutes and not more than two hours.
- Choose whatever issue is up for you at this point. I find the issues choose me. Sometimes I will get angry or become despondent and I know it's time to let some of it go.
- Start by writing with an intention that you are writing to express your feelings, anger, and frustration, whatever negativity is present. Nothing is off limits. Keep writing. Disregard spelling, punctuation, and penmanship BECAUSE YOU WILL NOT BE READING IT. Just write about it. It is a catharsis, a cleansing and a "no-holds-barred" exercise.
- When you finally write down all of your feelings and emotions or reach the end of your designated time, collect the sheets. Find a safe place to burn them. I burn mine in my fireplace, but I have also used a pan in the sink. Sometimes I first tear them into pieces, but as you watch the pages go up in smoke, the writing experience becomes a powerful energetic release as well as being a metaphor for the unconscious to release the old and make room for the new and the positive.
- I find that if I write long enough (not going over two hours), I will arrive at a place of calm in the writing process. When this happens, and it will

at some point although it doesn't always happen right away, there is a pearl of wisdom that comes forward and I will write that down separately. Stopping, I know that I have processed the worst of it, so I will take my journal out and record the nuggets of what I learned that evolved out of the purging.

I treat the pages I have written with the negativity that is attached to them as if they are radioactive and burn them as soon as possible. If I feel the need to enhance the clearing even more, I work on forgiveness of the negativity I've been feeling.

I like to meditate after this exercise as a means of tapping into inner peace, which is sweet and very deeply calming. I feel like I am absolutely ready to talk to God without negativity or self-recriminations. Nothing except peace remains when I allow myself to go through the complete process and then if I don't meditate, I will go for a walk through the trees to soothe my soul. If you are a runner, go for a run. Dancers, put on some soulful music and move . . . and like William W. Purkey said, "You've gotta dance like there's nobody watching."

There is nothing that free form writing can't make better and there is never any judgment or backlash, only pure release. It is like setting everything that is not you, on fire, and setting yourself free, emotionally, so you can return to your true self, restored. Then you can resume your life with greater peace and loving.

I created what I call the Fairy Godmother's Code. Although it reads much like a prayer or affirmation of what it is to live life as a Fairy Godmother, it is a template of our service to ourselves and the world.

"The Fairy Godmother Code"

Beloved Fairy Godmother within, help me to know that I am my own unique expression of giving and receiving love unconditionally. Guide me in all that I do in the name of love. I begin now with trust in the power of love to transform myself and my world. All that I am is my living prayer for myself and my beautiful world.

I am a spiritual mentor through encouragement and acceptance. I look for the good, see past the fear and separation and into the heart of a person or situation. I love and care for myself and I am peaceful and calm so that I may give from my overflow.

I know life is messy and so I keep a sense of humor never taking myself or anyone else too seriously. I look for the joy of living wherever I find myself. I let go of expectations and surrender to the miracles of perfect timing and divine guidance, knowing that miracles are afoot. I smile often and speak kind words to myself and others. I am grateful for all opportunities to extend a kind word or deed knowing that love is the answer and prayer works even though they may be silent ones. I am confident in the knowledge that prayers are seeds of loving and light that will do their job once I set them in motion through my intention.

I am filled with a divine sense of purpose as I hold the vision of the positive and abundant. I see the innocence of every soul regardless of their outer expression. When there is distress, I recognize that it is a cry for love. I ask for the highest good to be brought forward, knowing that all beings are beloved of God. I take nothing personal nor do I "take sides." I know that my intention is to be a channel for God's healing love and that visualization empowered by love, has the power to transform any condition.

I replace self-doubt with my sense of purpose to love where and when needed including myself. Judgment of myself or others is quickly dissolved in forgiveness and letting go, setting all free to come back into peace and harmony. I give myself and others the benefit of the doubt, embracing the idea that people are doing the best they can with what they know at any given moment while maintaining my own boundaries and that acceptance is a powerful force for transformation and loving.

I know that my thoughts and prayers have the power to transform. I am a good listener. I hold the attitude of gratitude for the fulfillment of miracles even before they manifest. When I am called to give some service or take on a project, I do so in the name of God and goodness, sharing in the flow of love and blessings of Light into the world.

This prayer or Code is a way of focusing on what it is to be a Fairy Godmother. You can read it as part of your morning practice, before your meditation or prayers, or before you fall asleep. If you read it daily, I guarantee it will make a place in your unconscious for more love. It may cause things that are not love to surface in your dreams or your feelings. At that point, I recommend free form writing to get it out where you can see it and let it go. No matter how you use it, it will lift you up.

These techniques and suggestions to nourish ourselves spiritually are designed to support us in building a reservoir of self-love and fill us with the Light that will sustain and protect us.

I encourage you to experience the truth of these experiences for yourself. There is no hurry, but I encourage you to be a participant in your own life. Allow your focus for these activities to be an inner one, one of connecting to your center. Through meditation, prayer, contemplation, and breathing techniques, you are entering into your inner territory, your true home.

One of the reasons for this is that God, the Beloved is already inside of you. When we center in our hearts, we are with God. God knows all the questions and has all the answers. If we need to have some guidance, we can go to the center of our being for direction, solace and love. In this way God colors the way we see our world, refreshes our tired eyes so that we can see beauty everywhere we look, see the preciousness of everyone we meet, see God in the sunset and the tiny flower that pushes up through the sidewalk. Connecting to God within us helps us to see God all around us wherever we are. The Beloved is the center of our being. All you need do is to awaken to it.

Here is my affirmation for this chapter:
I am embracing myself as the Beloved and surrendering to more love in the world.

Questions to deepen your awareness:
1. What person, place or experience opens your heart?
2. What are you grateful for?
3. Write about an experience where you were intuitively guided, guided by the Divine.
4. Who do you need to forgive?
5. Write about an experience where you knew you were loved unconditionally.
6. What is one thing you could change inside yourself that would allow more love in?

Chapter 12

Willingness to Do
Brings Ability to Do

"A willing heart is the key to possibilities; a person with a willing heart can do a lot of things that were declared as being impossible"

~ DJ Kyos

Willingness refers to how likely someone would be to do something whether it is a difficult or pleasant thing. **Ability** on the other hand is knowing what you are capable of and your competency to do something.

So here we are at the jumping off point of *willingness to do*. Are we going to courageously step into new territory leaving our old life behind and with the magic of saying *"yes"* step into a new world full of love and peace in the making? Ours is a world where we do not sit idly by and complain, but we step up and start *doing*. Will you have the courage to step into your Fairy Godmother self and begin the journey of change for the purpose of personal and world transformation?

Creating a new world of love, peace, and kindness begins with making a *choice*. At any given moment, will you choose to take the high road of faith, trust and *doing* and follow through on it? Or will it be a default choice of old patterns and habits that can take you down the road of self-doubt, separation, and apathy.

Upward Spiral of Faith and Trust

"Sometimes you have to believe before you can see."

~ WALT DISNEY

To me **faith** means believing in myself and believing that God, my higher power and *"creator of all things"* will answer my call to create what I want and need. **Trust** to me means that I trust in the process of creativity. If I have a clear intention, apply myself, and see the vision of it manifested, it will show up. With my willingness to participate, step-by-step, it happens. I hope that you too have, by now, caught the vision of a more loving, peaceful, and kind world; one where you are willing to be part of the solution of creating that kind of world.

Don't be the one who takes the downward road, buying into the idea that you are only one person and think that you can't do anything about the violence and disparity in the world.

I'm here to say that even just one person in a community can make a difference. Remember the story of the starfish? One person started out making a difference, then another joined in and, for all we know, if we were to continue the story, everyone on the beach that day, did their part and all the starfish were saved. The vision we want to see is one of a loving and more peaceful world.

Downward Spiral of Self-Doubt and Separation

Most of us know what it's like when life challenges us and what we thought was true about ourselves or someone else wound up falling short. As we all know, life takes us on so many different journeys; some good and some not so good; some even disastrous, but one thing we know for certain is that life is not *certain.*

What can we do when we think we are losing our grip on reality, dreams, goals, and aspirations? Sometimes we need a little guidance, a helping hand, or reassurance that we are going in the right direction when we are so easily side-tracked. How many times have you heard that if you keep a positive attitude, all good things will happen?

It's nearly impossible to keep a positive outlook when it feels as if everything is falling apart. Studies tell us that your mind can send you into deep, dark depths of chaos to that place where you doubt yourself, so your mind can also do just the opposite.

"Faith and fear both demand you believe
in something you cannot see, you choose."

~ BOB PROCTOR

We might feel inadequate and overwhelmed by expectations and experiences and sink into the doldrums of apathy, depression and despair, however the spiral has two directions. The choice is yours and *going up* is a good direction for the elevator of life.

When difficult times are upon you and it seems impossible to hold on to your dream because you are losing faith in yourself, **stop.** Just stop and catch yourself before you fall even deeper into that downward spiral. Again, you have a choice to *catch yourself and pull yourself up into a bigger and better story such as the hero's journey.* For us, it is a joyful, but potent tale where Fairy Godmothers and Beary Godfathers unite because they are out there always performing their small acts of kindness, caring and sharing.

They might be at home, sending light or planting light columns and saying prayers of harmony and peace when they hear or see distressful occurrences. That is also the job of the Fairy Godmother, holding the vision of the greater good and deeper peace. This is how we also come together into *one accord*, though miles and time zones may separate us. We know that love is the greatest power of all so we don't give our power away to the violence. We give our love to the vision of peace in the world. We surrender to the peace within us. Love is our connecting web and all beings are affected by love, plants, animals, the weather, all life is connected by love.

There are two basic motivating forces: fear and love. When we are afraid, we pull back from life. When we are in love, we are open to all that life has to offer with passion, excitement, and acceptance. In loving ourselves, first, in all our glory and imperfections, we can genuinely give of ourselves to others.

I have a story of a time when I had to overcome my own fear. I love horses, still do, but I no longer ride. My favorites are the Appaloosa horses. They are a traditional Native American horse, originally bred by the Nez Perce Indians. The horses' eyes, characteristically, look almost human because they have white sclera around their big brown eyes. They also have spots on their bodies, either on their rumps or all over their hides. I found a beautiful Appaloosa horse for sale in my neighborhood. Her name was Hiawatha. Ironically, when I was a child, one of my favorite books was a golden book about "Hiawatha" and I read it so many times that I wore it out. I would daydream about the pictures of the lake and visualize Hiawatha gliding along in his canoe, and his grandmother, Nakomis, on the shore of the Gitchigumi.

My horse, Hiawatha, was my pride and joy. She had white and black mottled fur with big black and white spots on her rump. Her silvery gray mane and tail were like an elders' hair. She had black socks and the black coloring around her eyes that extended out from her eyes as if she was wearing Egyptian makeup. She was a beauty with plenty of spirit. I was to find out how much spirit when I finally got to take her home. It was a two mile ride down the back hills from where she was stabled back to my place.

I visited her every Sunday riding her around the yard, feeding and brushing her. We had a very special bond. I did this for six months while making small payments every week until she was paid for. Although $500 was a lot of money for a waitress with four kids and working part-time in 1977, it was love at first sight for me and Hiawatha.

When the day finally arrived to take her home, we were going along fine for the first mile and I finally got her across the highway onto the trail. The farther away from her old home, however, the more agitated she became until it became an all-out war to keep her from throwing me off her, completely. She kept rearing up and eventually hit me right, square in the face. My nose started to bleed, profusely. We were a spectacle and people just stared at us along the way. I was shaking and so scared. I managed not to cry, but I had to be completely watchful to avoid being bumped again. I also feared that she might try running back home across a very fast highway and possibly kill us both.

I finally got her home and put her in the paddock and that is where she stayed. I fed and watered her, but I was too scared to ride her, again. A short time later, I realized that $500 was entirely too much money to be standing around doing nothing for the rest of our lives. So, one Saturday, I saddled her up. I got what we lovingly refer to as a "brain chain," which is a band that goes around the horse's ears, across the top of her head and down. From there, it hooked onto the cinch on the saddle to prevent her head from being thrown upward again where I already had one nose injury. It didn't hurt the horse, but it did have its restrictions. She could still buck, which is something she liked to do as I found out.

I walked her down to the end of the block and got into the deep sand of the wash which led under the highway to the big horse park and recreational area near my house. I climbed aboard while the heavy sand weighed her down. She couldn't really bounce around as before. I made her walk. I was still somewhat shaky, but my intention was to ride her and show her I could be trusted to guide her, which is what horses want. They want to know that you can handle them even when they're upset. They count on you having a "cool head." Geldings are much easier to handle, but I wanted a mare. I'd decided if I couldn't ride her, I would sell her.

We got to an open space with very deep sand. I started loping her around in the figure 8. I stopped her, started her, backed her up and, eventually, she began to respond without fighting me at every command. We continued until I was able to gallop with her in a larger figure "8." The wind was blowing through my hair and her mane, we became one. She surrendered and did exactly as I asked. All of a sudden, this ecstatic energy filled me completely. I felt this amazing sense of joyful power that I have only experienced one other time and that was walking on fire with Tony Robbins, years later.

After that, we were the best of friends and I knew in my heart and soul that Hiawatha was mine. I felt so empowered for what I accomplished. It made a big change in my life. I began to express myself more authentically and felt more joy more often.

This is what I call transforming fear into power. To me, fear is just unconverted power. This power resides in everyone. Every time we face something that we fear and do it anyway, it becomes our power.

Willingness to Be Will Lead to Doing More

1. Look for the good in yourself and then you'll easily find it in other people.
2. Wear a smile because smiles are contagious.
3. One of my favorite things is to *pay it forward*. When someone does something nice for you, besides responding with gratitude, you can spread the joy by extending the same kindness to others. What a wonderful world it would be if we all did this.
4. Keep a sense of humor and be prepared to laugh at yourself and don't take yourself so seriously.
5. Look for angels and believe in the possibilities of miracles.
6. Express gratitude whether it's to the mailman or a co-worker. When you say thank you to someone, look into their eyes as you say it, connect to their souls. Gratitude will always come back to you and enhance your heart health.
7. Plant the seeds of love. You can be the difference in small ways by offering someone help and hope.
8. Be the go-to person for your friends and co-workers by being generous with your time to listen or share a kind word or volunteer.
9. Practice forgiveness and set the example by being the first to apologize.
10. Be yourself and others will have permission to be themselves, demonstrate acceptance.

I am reminded of the story of "Two Wolves," which is a Cherokee legend. It depicts the two natures within us—the positive and the negative. It's about choices and how we can make them.

Story of Two Wolves

A young boy was struggling with his friendship with another boy, they always seemed to be competing for a place of honor among their peers. So, the boy finally went to his grandfather to ask his advice.

The grandfather took the boy into the forest where the wolves gathered. Wolves are very intelligent animals, he said, that live in packs and roam the open spaces to forage for food.

The boy asked his grandfather what he could do about the other boy and how not give into the anger that cut at his insides. Grandfather proceeded to tell him the story of the two wolves.

One wolf wanted to be known as a leader but frequently attacked his brothers, while the other wolf was very wise and a true leader, who didn't get caught up in the competition. When the evil wolf turned on the good wolf, the wise leader chose a different path.

Grandfather explained to the boy that everyone has an angry wolf and a calm wolf inside of them. The boy asked, "What do I do with the two wolves inside of me?" Grandfather said simply, "feed the good wolf, keep it close to you, don't feed the angry wolf and trust your instincts to take you in the right direction."

Our choice is always to feed our mind with faith and trust that we will be supported along the way of our divine intention, not feed into the fear and self-doubt.

A Fairy Godmother's instincts will be somewhere in the realm of traveling the positive road of believing in herself and her willingness to be of service and that willingness will open the path of ability. She will show up and what she can do will reveal itself and the power of love will infuse her with all she will need to fulfill her Fairy Godmother service.

> *"Bring your awareness to the truth that you are the blessings,*
> *follow and choose the loving as best you can."*
>
> – JOHN MORTON, DSS

Maybe it won't be *perfect* the first time, but as she leans into action, with a sense of playfulness and joy and a clear intention to do good, the transformation of loving will become real. She will feed the good wolf with her **soul food** and her vision of positivity and success.

I believe that every one of us has the capacity to be a Fairy Godmother or Beary Godfather. I trust that you enjoyed reading my stories and take my techniques and vision to heart, knowing that we each make a difference worldwide.

Our affirmation for this chapter:
I am courageously trusting my open loving heart and sharing my joy unconditionally.

Questions to deepen your awareness:
1. Write about an experience you had where you did something you were afraid to do regardless of your fear.
2. Make a list of five positive statements that apply to your life.
3. What really scares me?
4. What are my courageous qualities?
5. What new task/experience in my life did I do with little or no training?
6. Make a list of your personal successes in life.

Chapter 13

A New World Full of Love

"If one is lucky, a solitary fantasy
can transform a million realities."

~ MAYA ANGELOU

Now the journey begins. You are not alone. Everywhere you look, a more universal love is being talked about, written about, or made into movies. What is the upward spiral for us as Fairy Godmothers and Beary Godfathers? It is our ability to see the greater good and we do this by participating in the creation of a more loving, kind and peaceful world.

We've been learning about what the requirements are for a Fairy Godmother. I shared my own story and my wish for more Fairy Godmothers in the world, which is more love and, yes, it was a complicated beginning that started it all. I know that many of you will have your own personal reasons for getting involved as well as your dream, like mine, for a better world.

We looked at the tools and how to take care of ourselves physically, mentally and emotionally. Then we learned how to take care of ourselves spiritually. We've looked closely at giving and receiving love and how to maintain our inner love. We've looked at techniques on how to connect to the Beloved and, in many ways, we've been preparing.

Now what? Now we find ourselves at the crossroads where we either choose to believe in the vision and step out into the world to begin our Fairy Godmother journey or we hang back and think to ourselves, *Oh that was a nice story but . . .*

A New Global Reality. Why Now? Why Not Now?

We have a greater ability to be global now. With the Internet, we are truly connecting, like a network, with more information than was ever possible at any other time in history. We can communicate to a mass audience, whether we speak their language or not. We also have the devastating ability to annihilate all human life on this planet with nuclear warfare and even germ warfare.

We've never had more potential to lift the world up or cast it down. To me, if there was ever a time to bring forward planetary peace and loving, it is now. We have the technology to do great harm, but we also have technology and new scientific breakthroughs and medical innovations to create great healing. We have discovered new sciences like Quantum Physics and Quantum Mechanics. These disciplines would have been seen in the past, as *pure magic*. Thanks to the pioneers of this kind of research about energy and matter and their relationships, it translates into a whole new way of living.

I'm going to share briefly some of the technology that I find to be particularly relevant to us in creating a more loving and peaceful world.

History has seen devastating wars every 30–50 years. Presently, it is the longest period of time that we have not had a war that effected many countries at one time. I for one would like to keep it that way and I believe that the lack of a world war says that we are ready to take the next leap into a more loving and peaceful world.

In fact, as a Fairy Godmother, I envision the world described by the lyrics of John Lennon: *"Imagine all the people living life in peace."* Lennon was a dreamer, *"but I'm not the only one,"* he said. I think it's time for the dream and Fairy Godmothers and Beary Godfathers everywhere to begin it. I think it's time to take the dream of peace and love into the 21st Century to make it real. The time is now.

As long as we're talking about time, let's look at some of the discoveries made by Dr. Hugh Everette III in 1957. Many of us tend to look at time in the linear way, going back into the past and forward into the future. There has been much research about time and some of it is very compelling and has been proven. Dr. Everette's research says that time is also vertical and exists in layers that he calls "parallel possibilities," and not just one, but many possible futures, all existing at the same time. Here's an example: Here we are in the present day, hurdling through time, toward destruction of our ecosystem, natural disasters from violent weather, not to mention possible warfare and disease, because of our current choices of how we interact with nature, economics, each other, etc. Parallel possibilities and vertical time suggest that we can choose another future. We can change our attitudes, our actions, and our priorities today. There is a different reality possible and it already exists, now. We can access the greater planetary good by shifting into a different outcome, a more balanced and harmonious world.

Because of the parallel possibilities of vertical time, we can create the conditions where disease, warfare, hate, natural disasters, NEVER HAPPEN. This is not a dream, quantum physics says it's a reality. What is the deciding factor? The choices we make in our lives **now.**

If you want more in-depth proof and information, read Gregg Braden's book, *The Isaiah Effect*. Depok Chopra, Steven Hawking, and Albert Einstein have been quoted on the subject of time as well. They all speak and write about the ramifications of quantum realities. The science of it all just confirms what we Fairy Godmothers and Beary Godfathers already know. We can transform our world through loving. I think that science, in its own way, is catching up to spiritual realities. The founder of Transcendental Meditation, the Maharishi Mahesh Yogi and inspirational writer said it best: *"Love is the glue that holds the universe together."* Peace allows more love to be present. Peace and love connected makes for a better life and better world.

So to me, it's time to make the choice to love and bring peace to all. If we want peace and love to prevail, we need to be busy choosing it, every day in how we live our life and especially for us Fairy Godmothers. It's what we are creating as we go out and do our random acts of kindness, carry the energy of peace and do loving, caring and sharing things throughout our world. It happens when we nourish our souls and connect to our own Beloved and share from the overflow.

I can't help but re-visit a wonderful message from the Bible that tells us when we choose love, peace, caring, sharing, compassion, joy and kindness, we are becoming a part of it. We create a new world when we choose a world full of love as well as greater peace.

"As a man thinketh in his heart, so he becomes."

~ PROVERBS

Speaking of the heart that brings me to the next scientific research that really supports us and enables us to navigate our stressful world. To have the presence of mind and heart to make the good choices, calm emotions, remain peaceful during times of stress and chaos. It's called HeartMath. The folks at the HeartMath Institute in Northern California have a whole learning model of how to access greater peace through breathing and connecting it to our hearts. I have a list of resources at the end of our final chapter so you can support yourself and support our world in some highly effective and loving ways that exist today.

Our hearts can and will play a big part in our life. We used to think the brain regulated everything, that the brain would send out a message and the nervous system would respond, etc. The HeartMath studies show that it is the heart center that is the biggest regulator of energy in our bodies. We can affect the heart through breathing into it, which has a brain of its own. It becomes the real regulator of energy for us

So, in some of the meditations, we will use breathing techniques through the heart to access our divine energy and then we will send it up to the mind to soothe thoughts and fears.

I learned from my classes with HeartMath that every major organ has a brain of its own and the head of it all is the brain that is around the heart. Think of it, we can use our breath to breathe love into ourselves and heal ourselves by bringing our energy into resonance. We can bring peace and connection, heart to heart, by focusing on our heart and communicating peace to others. Again, this is another way we can affect the world around us and create peace and love to realize a beautiful future for us all.

This brings me to the power of meditation and prayer. In 1975, Transcendental Meditation (TM) was brought to America by Maharishi Mahesh Yogi and with this technique for meditation came new data about the power of meditation. Numerous studies were done all over the world including America. The effects of TM transcended the overall social climate and activities in any area where this meditation was going on.

The study was conducted in different cities where one percent of the population practiced TM, meditated, for 30 minutes in the morning and 30 minutes in the evening. What they found was that it took only one percent of the population participating to create a change. Violent crime, domestic violence dropped at least 30 percent and the stock market rose and stayed up for as long as the meditation took place. When the meditation stopped, the previous levels of violence returned and the stock market also came down.

In 1970, in Los Angeles, the Spiritual Center known as PRANA, Purple Rose Ashram of the New Age, founded by John-Roger, also documented that although the center was in an impoverished area in mid-Los Angeles, within one year of opening, there was a reported drop in crime and violence. Its members living at the spiritual center meditated constantly, morning and evening.

They have done blind studies in hospitals and recovery centers where half of the patients recovering from heart disease and other surgeries were prayed for everyday by volunteers participating in the study. Those who were prayed for had faster and sometimes fuller recoveries than those who weren't included. In some cases there were even complications for those left out of prayers compared to those who were prayed for.

Greg Braden mentions in one of his books, *The Lost Art of Prayer*, that other ancient texts speak of certain information about how to pray and the power of seeing your prayer fulfilled. At the end of this chapter I offer re-sources for some of the organizations I have mentioned, books, and their authors.

Finding Your Tribe

Life's more fun with a buddy. Get a friend to buddy up with you and share the experience of being a Fairy Godmother or Beary Godfather wherever you go, whatever your experience. Check in with each other and make a date to get together for lunch or dinner to share the fun of getting out there. If you are one of us that doesn't get out as much, call a buddy and talk about what you did that day to practice Fairy Godmothering.

When you can't get out much or at all, there is still much to be done from wherever you are. When you watch or listen to the news on TV or surf the Web and hear about disturbing situations, stop and call in the Light for yourself and then send it to that place in need. You can also place Light columns just like I taught you.

Always support yourself and journal your experiences so you can celebrate and learn. There will be times when it may seem awkward, so writing your feelings will reveal little things about the experience; a way of refining your next trip out. When you have those feelings of exhilaration, inspiration, sheer joy for being of service, write about it. You can put all the really good juicy stuff in one journal and "room for improvement/learning." in a different journal.

Another thing about a buddy or a few buddies is that you can get together for a book study on the material in the book. Share your feelings, wins, or talk about what you've read and each person's realizations and celebrations of awareness. Ask the pastor of your church to have a mini-workshop on the material. Many churches, thank God, have outreach programs and this is a great outreach because it's fun and community-building.

Make a pact with your buddy to email or call at least once a week to compare notes, inspire and encourage each other and above all celebrate each other. Since meditating in a group can change the energy of your neighborhood, you might want to get together and meditate with your buddy/buddies or set a specific time when you can all be together to meditate. See the meditations in Chapter 11 and if you want more guidance on meditating, the *www.MSIA.org* website has information available. I have found the MSIA meditations very effective. They offer different techniques. The book *The Rest of Your Life*, by John-Roger, comes with a CD of several meditations.

Keeping Momentum through
Inspiration and Community

It's so easy to receive information, read a good book, put it down, and move on. I ask you, move on to what? When you picked up this book out of many, there was a reason, and it probably had to do with living in a better and more loving world. You caught the vision, even if only for the period of time it took you to read the book. I am inviting you to keep the magic going. Join the community of Fairy Godmothers and Beary Godfathers and start looking around where you live or work and find ways to participate by doing random acts of kindness, being a good listener, sending and placing Light columns when you see or hear disturbing situations in our communities or world.

Human beings are lovers of inspiration. We can take advantage of this by seeing inspirational movies, reading or participating in a book study. The movie industry is huge and, when at its best, it shows social commentary through the magic of film, addresses current day issues, and suggests more inspirational outcomes. I would love to see the movie industry get much larger than the war industry, not for any political reasons, but just because we wouldn't need it if there were no more wars! Give our armed forces other jobs to do such as building shelters and low income housing for struggling families, cleaning up the environment, rebuilding after natural disasters. I know that some will say that this is a nice idea, but it all starts with one step in the right direction.

No matter who you are, your current mobility, you can make a difference just by your intention and a little time and forethought throughout your day. We talked about the qualities of a Fairy Godmother, i.e., F-faith, A-acceptance and awareness, I-Intention and inspiration, R-right place/right time and risking, and finally Y-you saying yes to love. So, now you have a template to use so opportunities can emerge.

Join together, whether it is with like-minded people, a friend or family member who wants to do things with you, or spending time with someone special. You could go out, drive around and find a homeless person to take food to. At the doctor's office, give someone the gift of your attention, volunteer at the library to read to small children or at a children's center, the Boys and Girls Clubs, visit the senior who lives down the block and chat a while, etc. There are so many ideas, but you probably have some of your own. I hope you will contact me with your thoughts or share with me what you are doing to make a more loving world.

You never need be all alone. Give yourself the gift of belonging. I am a professional storyteller and we have a professional guild. In our community of storytellers, we make every effort to get together. Some say that getting storytellers all together is not unlike *herding cats*. If you are like me, become a Fairy Godmother and Beary Godfather. We are a fun-loving, loosely wrapped fellowship. Gather people together to participate with you from your group of friends, family, or church. Even if you find yourself alone, you can have your own timing and do *Light work* by yourself in your own home. There is no wrong way to commit to doing something positive and thoughtful. Doing nothing will never carry positive results. People of every age have been creating love and peace in our neighborhoods, but more is needed. **It is never too late**. Young or old, surely we all have the energy to squeeze in a single random act of kindness each day. Age or circumstances should not prevent anyone from doing "good." With a positive attitude of cooperation, use your social media to connect and share your projects and their success or your willingness to serve, love and be kind. There is no quota, there is no "end result" to fall short of, and there is only a world full of heartfelt loving, caring, sharing, kindness, peace and joy.

To be a Fairy Godmother or Beary Godfather, you must believe in the power of love. I offer these techniques and practices and words of encouragement and support so that you will be prepared, loved, and divinely guided and protected as you go forward, into the world, and create a kinder, more loving and peaceful existence for yourself and your children and grandchildren to come; a world where everyone matters. If you join me, the least of what could happen is that you could have more peace, self-love, and balance to deal with your own life, but first we must be open to more love. Who could ever say that they have too much love?

"Love is the opening door, love is what we came here for,
no one could offer you more, do you know what I mean . . ."

~ ELTON JOHN

Think of it, Fairy Godmothers, in every neighborhood, reaching out through acts of kindness, caring and sharing. Holding the Light, and creating peace through meditation. I do, I think about it every day and in my spirit I am reaching out to all of you who might hear the call and I am sending you love and light, believing in you, holding the vision, knowing we can make a difference.

My profound hope and prayer for you is to be embraced by the love of your inner Beloved and know a deep peace and sense of purpose and never lose sight of the vision of **more love in the world**.

About the Author

Diana Spirithawk, DSS, (Doctor of Spiritual Science) is a storyteller, inspirational speaker, world-renowned artisan of Native American Ceremonial art, a dream interpreter and educator. She has been sharing her mission to create a better world through storytelling for more than 30 years. Diana uses her inspiration to make soulful connections. A spiritual mentor by her very nature, she is a true Fairy Godmother.

Diana earned her doctorate at Peace Theological Seminary & College of Philosophy (PTS) and has been an ordained minister of Light through the Movement of Spiritual Inner Awareness (MSIA) for more than 40 years. Spirithawk, as her students and Mother Earth friends call her, was a road woman for six years, traveling extensively to learn the spiritual ways of the indigenous people of North America. She received her name "Spirithawk" through a mysterious and prophetic dream in 1991. Her name means "messenger of spirit" and that is surely what she does through storytelling, dream work, and writing.

Diana resides in California with her husband, David, and their three dogs. *Handbook for Fairy Godmothers: Transforming Our Lives through Loving* is Diana's first book and her second book is already on the drawing board. She has also recorded an original story, *Legend of the Star Kachina,* available on CD.

To contact Diana for speaking engagements, storytelling, spiritual coaching, send an email to: MyFairyGM@gmail.com

Resources

Website and Online Support

GLCoherence.Org—Global network for sending energy of peace to other places in the world as well as our own.

HeartMath.Org—Classes, information on the science of heart resonance and its benefits and practice.

MSIA.Org—MSIA Products Department for books and audios for spiritual support.

MSIA.Org/quotes—"Loving Each Day" a free online daily email quote offered for spiritual support.

"Super Soul Sunday"—Oprah Winfrey on OWN Channel.

Recommended Reading

Big Leap, Gay Hendricks, HarperOne

Inspiration: Finding Your True Calling, Dr. Wayne Dyer, HayHouse

The Power of Intention, Dr. Wayne Dyer, HayHouse

Loving Each Day, Loving Each Day for Peace Makers, The Spiritual Warrior, The Rest of Your Life: Finding Repose in the Beloved, Forgiveness: Keys to the Kingdom, John-Roger, DSS, Mandeville Press

Loyalty to the Soul, Ronald and Mary Hulnick, HayHouse

Saying Yes to Life, Betsy Gutting, New Bloom Press

Secrets of the Lost Mode of Prayer, The Isaiah Effect, Gregg Braden, HayHouse

The Return to Love, Marianne Williamson, HarperOne

From Tears to Triumph, Marianne Williamson, Harper Perennial

I would love to hear from you about what you are doing, send an email to me at MyFairyGM@gmail.com or visit www.HandbookForFairyGodmothers.com

CPSIA information can be obtained
at www.ICGtesting.com
Printed in the USA
LVOW10s0818020517
532927LV00032B/2186/P